# The Cassandra Complex

Marie-Louise von Franz, Honorary Patron

**Studies in Jungian Psychology
by Jungian Analysts**

Daryl Sharp, General Editor

# The Cassandra Complex

## Living with Disbelief

### A Modern Perspective on Hysteria

**LAURIE LAYTON SCHAPIRA**

To my mother and her mother and all other unmothered mothers.

**Canadian Cataloguing in Publication Data**

Schapira, Laurie Layton, 1949-
  The Cassandra complex

(Studies in Jungian psychology by Jungian analysts; 36)

Bibliography: p.
Includes index.

ISBN 0-919123-35-X

1. Women—Psychology.  2. Hysteria.  3. Cassandra (Greek
mythology).  4. Hysteria—Treatment.  5. Jung, C.G.
(Carl Gustav), 1875-1961.  I. Title.  II. Series.

HQ1206.S34 1988        155.6'33        C88-094501-X

INNER CITY BOOKS
Box 1271, Station Q, Toronto, Canada M4T 2P4
Telephone (416) 927-0355

Honorary Patron: Marie-Louise von Franz.
Publisher and General Editor: Daryl Sharp.
Senior Editor: Victoria Cowan.
Editorial Board: Fraser Boa, Daryl Sharp, Marion Woodman.
Production: David Sharp.

INNER CITY BOOKS was founded in 1980 to promote the
understanding and practical application of the work of C.G. Jung.

*Cover:* The Woman with the Skeletons (Lady Macbeth), 1906, by
Gustav-Adolf Mossa (1883-1971).

Index by Daryl Sharp.

Printed and bound in Canada by Webcom Limited

# Contents

*See final page for descriptions of other Inner City Books*

# Acknowledgments

I wish to thank Don Kalsched for being ruthless in such a related way, and, for their insightful feedback, Philip Zabriskie, Sylvia Perera and especially Gertrude Ujhely.

Additional thanks go to Stephanie Woodbridge, editor; Sharon Abner, typist; Doris Albrecht, librarian at the C.G. Jung Foundation in New York; Nathan Schwartz-Salant, for believing me; and Beverley Zabriskie, for her ongoing support.

But most of all, I want to thank Peter Lynn for his abiding love.

Working on this book confirmed once again that there's nothing new under the sun. It was truly a medial experience during which I took in data not just by academic research but also via the collective unconscious, through my psychic pores. Therefore, I wish to acknowledge, with thanks, those whose influence remains below the surface of my conscious awareness but who nonetheless helped bring this work to fruition.

*The sky is falling. . . . Run, folks, run!*
—Chicken Little.


*The fate of warnings in political affairs is to be futile
when the recipient wishes to believe otherwise.*
—Barbara Tuchman, *The March of Folly: From Troy to Vietnam.*


*A burning tripod bids you be aware,
The deep of deeps at last awaits you there.*
—Goethe, *Faust.*

# Introduction

I became interested in the subject of Cassandra when two of my analysands dreamed about her. Looking for shared psychological patterns, I found many commonalities, not the least of which was a strong hysterical component to their personalities.

Hysteria is no longer a popular diagnosis. In fact, it has been deleted from the most recent edition of the American Psychiatric Association's *Diagnostic and Statistical Manual of Mental Disorders* (DSM III) as a diagnostic category on its own. Yet hysteria still exists as a well-defined clinical entity, even though we tend to shy away from making a diagnosis with such misogynist, chauvinistic connotations. We prefer to attribute exhibitionistic tendencies to a "narcissistic personality disorder" or emotional outbursts to a "borderline condition."

Nearly a century ago, Pierre Janet stated:

> The word "hysteria" should be preserved, although its primitive meaning has much changed. It would be very difficult to modify it nowadays, and truly it has so great and beautiful a history that it would be painful to give it up.[1]

Perhaps the same can be said for the diagnosis of hysteria, which has been a documented reality for four thousand years. Much has been written about this disease in the patriarchal era. Here we will look at this history from a feminist point of view and with a constructive eye to the teleology of its symptoms, seeking to understand its modern significance.

The woman I identify as having a Cassandra complex exhibits a specific hysterical pattern, including a marked split in the personality. On the face of it, the Cassandra woman is well adapted in an extraverted way: bright, active, competent, responsible, even compulsive about what she does, as well as capable of sustaining long-term, if somewhat superficial, relationships. But at times her persona sud-

---

[1] *The Mental State of Hystericals: A Study of Mental Stigmata and Mental Accidents* (New York: Putnam & Sons, 1901), p. 527.

9

denly falls apart, leaving a frightened, needy little girl, wanting to be
taken care of but unable to express her needs or find her way in the
black chaos of the unconscious. She has no guide, no containment;
she is helpless, hopeless, terrified.

In Jungian terms, we see an animus-identified ego which is split
off from, and erected largely in defense against, a powerful negative
mother complex. The ego, a caricature of Apollo—dedicated to, yet
bound by, order, reason, truth and clarity—disavows itself of anything dark and irrational. This is Apollo in his misogynist aspect
who, according to Aeschylus, said:

> The mother to the child that men call hers
> Is no true life-begetter, but a nurse
> Of live seed. 'Tis the sower of the seed
> Alone begetteth. Woman comes at need,
> A stranger, to hold safe in trust and love
> That bud of new life—save when God above
> Wills that it die. . . .
> There have been fathers where no mother is.[2]

Referring to these lines, James Hillman writes:

> We do not know why Apollo made the speech or why Aeschylus put
> it in his mouth. It is a statement of an archetypal position repre-
> senting a world-view which can be attributed to Apollo and may be
> called Apollonic.[3]

Our culture is informed by Apollonic consciousness. Identified as
we are with the positive value of this viewpoint, it may be difficult to
see Apollo in a negative light. Nonetheless, he casts a very dark
shadow.

His abusive, rapacious attitude toward the feminine is well
known. This is the same Apollo who usurped the Delphic oracle
from the earth goddess, never acknowledging the oracle's matriarchal
roots. He pays homage to the feminine only insofar as he needs a
woman to inspire with his divine madness. But he is most ruthless
when his chosen is unfaithful or spurns him, as did Cassandra. He
bestowed upon her his gift of prophecy. But when she refused to

---

2 *The Eumenides*, lines 659-666.
3 *The Myth of Analysis,* p. 225.

consummate their union, he added a curse to his gift: that no one would ever believe her.

Here is an aborted *coniunctio*. Cassandra refused Apollo. Why? We will analyze the character and motivation of both Cassandra and Apollo. In exploring Cassandra's psychodynamics and the reasons for her tragic end, we hope to find some other resolution to her terrible conflict and suggest a more creative lysis in the lives of her modern-day counterparts.

We will look closely at the Cassandra myth, its manifestation in the feminine psyche today and its relevance to hysteria. When a woman falls into her hysterical shadow, her breathless ravings have a quality similar to Cassandra's bloody prophecies of doom and gloom. What she sees and experiences in this state may have potential value and contain more than a grain of truth; but what she says is not believed because it is so ungrounded. This shadowy insight is cut off from the perspective of ego-consciousness and the clarifying objectivity of the Apollonian animus. Even *she* does not believe what she sees.

I shall also present a psychological profile of the modern Cassandra woman. On the basis of this profile, I shall discuss therapeutic implications and describe the clinical phases of the analytic process. This involves disidentification of ego from animus and the consequent transformation of both. The feminine ego, once grounded in a Self-syntonic matrix, can integrate the Cassandrian shadow. And the Apollonian animus can function positively as inspiration and light-giver. Only then can Cassandra and Apollo achieve their longed-for *coniunctio*.

Apollo shooting the Python.
(Roman coin, ca. 5th cent. B.C.)

# Part One
# Cassandra Then

Cassandra being attacked by Clytemnestra.
(Attic vase; Mansell Collection, London)

# 1

# The Myth and Tragedy of Cassandra

*O woe. O woe, woe!*
*The torment of seeing sweeps me away again.*
— Cassandra, in Christa Wolf, *Cassandra.*

Cassandra was one of the daughters of Priam and Hecuba, the king and queen of Troy. One day while she was in the temple of Apollo, the god appeared and promised her the art of prophecy if she would lie with him. After accepting his gift, Cassandra refused to fulfill her part of the bargain.

It is said that divine favors once bestowed cannot be revoked. So Apollo begged Cassandra to give him one kiss and, as she did so, he breathed (some say spat) into her mouth, thus insuring that no one would believe her prophecies.

From the beginning of the Trojan War, Cassandra foretold its gloomy end. But no one ever listened to her predictions. She pronounced that the Greeks were hiding in the wooden horse, but the Trojans would not heed her warnings. It was her fate to know what disasters were coming and be unable to avert them.

Cassandra was won by Agamemnon as a spoil of war. When he brought her back to Mycenae, they were greeted by Clytemnestra, Agamemnon's wife, who had conspired with her lover, Aegisthus, to murder them both. Cassandra sensed her doom and refused to enter the palace. Caught in a prophetic trance, crying that she smelled blood, she felt the full weight of the curse on the House of Atreus. But she could not avoid her fate. Clytemnestra killed her with the same ax with which she beheaded Agamemnon.[1]

---

[1] Compiled from Robert Graves, *The Greek Myths,* vol. 2, pp. 51-56, 263-264; Edith Hamilton, *Mythology,* pp. 202, 243-244; *Larousse Encyclopedia of Mythology,* p. 118.

15

Cassandra is a tragic figure. Her story has been the subject of Greek drama, poetry and even an opera. In literature, tragedy is a result of a flaw in the character of the tragic figure whereby some great potential goes unfulfilled, even turns destructive. What then is the nature of Cassandra's tragedy?

When Cassandra refused to consummate their union, Apollo cursed her so that her prophecies would never be believed. But why did she refuse him? Was she simply not interested in him? The story indicates otherwise. In *The Agamemnon,* Cassandra describes their foreplay: "We wrestled, and his breath to me was sweet." Only when it "came to the getting of children, as is meet," she "swore a lie."[2]

Was she trying to get something for nothing? Was she being a sexual tease, like many an hysteric? Certainly, also in the manner of the hysteric, Cassandra was ambivalent. At first she complied and then she reneged. Perhaps her ambivalence also held some passive aggression: anger at Apollo for his past outrages toward the feminine, and a fear of being abused and abandoned as had happened to so many other objects of his desire.

Apollo was in effect calling Cassandra to be his Pythia, "the God's bride," to be filled with his divine inspiration.[3] In the process of divination, the Pythia was known to become "*entheos, plena deo:* the god entered into her and used her vocal organs as if they were his own."[4]

Historically, the woman chosen at Delphi to be this sacred vessel for the god had to have a good moral character, absolute integrity and an earthy solidity. She had to come from a sound, respected, but simple family and to have led an irreproachable life so that when she approached the god she would do so with a truly virgin heart. Diodorus Siculus states that "in ancient times oracles were pronounced by virgins, by virtue of their physical purity and association with Artemis; on which account they were readier to keep secret the oracles they revealed."[5]

---

[2] Aeschylus, *The Agamemnon,* lines 1206-1208.

[3] Robert Flacelière, *Greek Oracles,* p. 42.

[4] E. R. Dodds, *The Greeks and the Irrational,* p. 70.

[5] Flacelière, *Greek Oracles,* pp. 41-42.

Even so, many a Pythia shattered under the strain. On some level, Cassandra may have known that she did not possess those attributes which the ancients, in their intuitive wisdom, set forth as requisites for the woman who acts as sacred vessel for the god.

Archetypally, the "vessel" is associated with the feminine, with a receptive capacity, the womb. On a personal level, a woman's psychological vessel is her ego. Cassandra had a weak vessel. This was her tragic flaw. She was not virgin in a psychological sense:

> The woman who is virgin, one-in-herself, does what she does—not because of any desire to please, not to be liked, or to be approved, even by herself; not because of any desire to gain power over another . . . but because what she does is true.[6]

In contrast, Cassandra, like the hysteric, would do anything to be loved. She ultimately said no to Apollo because it was the only way she could survive in the face of the overwhelming power of the masculine. Unfortunately, Cassandra was not able to refuse Apollo more consciously and directly, even confront him on his rapacious, misogynistic shadow. Through such an act she would have claimed her feminine reality and established her virginity, which would eventually enable her to fulfill her destiny as sacred vessel for the god.

But Cassandra did not have the ego strength. She had a deeply afflicted relationship to the feminine, thus her ego was insufficiently grounded in the feminine matrix. As we shall see in the next chapter, there were many reasons for this, both personal and collective.

---

[6] M. Esther Harding, *Woman's Mysteries,* p. 125.

Two aspects of Apollo.
*Left:* Apollo Veii.
(Terra cotta, ca. 510 B.C.; Museo Nazionale di Villa Giulia, Rome)
*Right:* Apollo Belvedere.
(Marble, ca. 4th to 1st cent. B.C.; Vatican Museum, Rome)

# 2

# Cassandra's Wounds

## Collective Dynamics

The collective factors affecting the historical Cassandra include the decline of the goddess as a supreme deity and an increasing reverence for Apollo. These issues also figure prominently in the historical development of what we now call the negative mother complex, which we shall look at in later chapters.

Here we will pay especially close attention to Apollo's evolution from his primitive to classical form. This serves as a paradigm for the development of the Cassandra woman's animus, her inner image of the masculine.

Cassandra's story took place during the Bronze Age in the second millennium B.C. At that time, the Greek world was undergoing a major upheaval, a transition from matriarchal to patriarchal culture with a consequent decline in feminine values. This change must have been particularly traumatic to the Trojans, whose culture was closer to the matriarchal Cretan/Minoan than the more patriarchal Achaean. When Troy was defeated by the Greeks, her culture and religion were displaced as well.

In her book *Cassandra,* East German writer Christa Wolf points out that in Troy, the worship of the new gods was being practiced alongside the ancient matriarchal cults. "At one seam of these conflict-ridden happenings stands Cassandra."[1] Certainly she would have been deeply affected by this transition to patriarchal worship, perhaps even more than other women of her time, since this transition would undermine the development of a strong feminine identity through reverence for the goddess as an archetypal role model.

Apollo was one such new god, although he was not so much new as changed in character. In his primitive form during the matriarchal

---

[1] *Cassandra,* p. 293.

period, Apollo was son-lover to the Great Mother. One of his earliest titles was Smintheus, who was originally an oracular mouse-god, Cretan in origin and worshiped in the goddess's shrine.[2] Likewise, Apollo is identified with Karu, son of the Cretan bee-goddess Car (Ceres). Karu was Megisthos Kouros, the year-king whose hair was shorn annually before his death.[3]

We commonly recognize Apollo as the son of Leto. What is not so well known is that Leto is a later form of Lat, the Palestinian triple moon goddess and another name for Isis. Thus Apollo is also identified with the child Horus, her son.[4] Classical scholar Lewis Farnell describes Leto as a she-wolf who gave birth to the aboriginal Apollo Lykeios. *Lykeian* means "the light of the howling wolf," that is, the moon.

In prehistoric Greece, the sun was subordinate to the moon and both were associated with the goddess. It was not until Mycenaean days that Apollo acquired his solar character. Apollo Lykeios was more in the nature of an earth daimon. He was savage and wild, a god of the chase, carrying his bow and arrows and haunting caves, grottos and wild woods. Together with the wolf, the raven and the crow were his holy animals. He was also a pastoral and vegetation god, more like Pan or Dionysus, whose rituals were marked by "frenzied possession and the ecstasy of wood-magic."[5]

We can see the face of this archaic Apollo on the Etruscan statue on page 18. According to Karl Kerényi, Italy encountered Apollo in his pre-Homeric form, since Italy was not influenced by Homer who first presented the Greek gods in their classical form. There, Apollo was a primitive, dark and fatal god until very late. He was worshiped as Soranus Pater, the lord of the underworld. "Even the knowing smile of Apollo of Veii—that admired 'Etruscan smile'—is a wolf's smile."[6]

As late as Homer, we see the dark face of Apollo as a terrible death-dealing god. The following description of Apollo appears at the

---

2 Graves, *Greek Myths,* vol. 1, p. 56.
3 Ibid., pp. 280, 327.
4 Ibid., p. 80.
5 *The Cults of the Greek States,* vol. 4, pp. 112-113, 123-124, 140.
6 *Apollo,* p. 56.

beginning of *The Iliad*. In fact, it is the first Apollonian epiphany in Greek literature:

> Down from the peaks of Olympus he strode angry in his heart,
> With his bow and doubly covered quiver on his shoulders.
> The arrows clattered on the shoulders of the angry god
> As he moved. He went like the night.
> Then he sat far from the ships and shot an arrow;
> And there was a terrible clang of the silver bow.
> First the mules and swift hounds it strikes,
> Then a weapon with its sharp edge aimed at the men
> He shoots; the corpse fires burned often and everywhere.[7]

According to Walter Otto, Apollo became "the god of purity only at a later period, and his sharp clarity, his superior spirit, his will that enjoins insight, moderation, and order, in short all that we call Apollonian to this day, must have been unknown to Homer."[8]

In *The Iliad*, Homer describes Apollo as he would have appeared at the time of the Trojan War and the historical Cassandra (circa 1200 B.C.): less the son-lover of the goddess and more the son of Zeus, although not yet in his purified later form.

Classical scholar Jane Harrison delineates Apollo's historical development through three phases: 1) prehistoric earth daimon, 2) transitional hero (Homeric), 3) Olympian sky-god. She traces the change in the relationship between Apollo and Artemis through these phases:

> In Homer a great effort is made to affiliate Artemis as one of the patriarchal family, but, in her ancient aspect . . . she is manifestly but a form of the Great Mother: at Delphi, where Apollo reigns supreme, his "sister" Artemis is strangely, significantly absent. What has happened is fairly obvious. Artemis, as mother, had a male-god as son or subordinate consort, just as Aphrodite had Adonis. When patriarchy ousted matriarchy, the relationship between the pair is first spiritualized as we find it in Artemis and Hippolytos; next the pair are conceived of in the barren relation of sister and brother. Finally the female figure dwindles altogether and the male-

---

[7] Ibid., p 39, quoting *The Iliad*, line 44.
[8] *The Homeric Gods*, p. 65.

consort emerges as merely son of his father or utterer of his father's will.[9]

Thus Artemis lost her supremacy as Magna Mater, although even into classical times she retained her pre-Hellenic character in Asia Minor. At shrines such as Ephesus, Magnesia and Iasos, sacrifices were made on her altar to the Pythian Apollo as her high priest.[10]

The development of Pythian Apollo also reflects the transition from matriarchy to patriarchy. The epithet Pythian refers to Apollo's very first heroic feat, the slaying of the serpent Python who guarded the shrine at Delphi, thus appropriating the oracle for himself.

But Delphi was a religious center during the matriarchy, long before it became sacred to Apollo. The origin of prophecy at Delphi is described by Diodorus Siculus:

At the spot where the *adyton* of the present temple is there was once a chasm in the ground, where before Delphi was yet a city the goats used to graze. Whenever one of them approached this chasm and looked down into it, she would begin leaping about in an amazing fashion and bleating in a quite different voice to her normal one. And when the shepherd, marvelling at this prodigious behavior, examined the chasm to find out what caused it, he himself was affected in the same way as the goats, who in truth behaved for all the world like people possessed, and began to prophesy the future. Later, news of what happened to those who visited the chasm began to spread among the peasants, and they flocked to the spot in large numbers, anxious to put the miracle to the test; and whenever one of them drew near he fell into a trance. Thus it was that the place itself became regarded as miraculous, and they believed that the oracle came to them from Gê, the Earth goddess. For a time, those who came thither to seek advice used to proclaim oracles to one another. But, later on, when many people in their ecstasy had hurled themselves into the chasm and disappeared, it seemed good to those who lived in those parts that, for the protection of others, one woman should be appointed as the sole prophetess, who alone should pronounce the oracles. They therefore constructed a device so that she could sit in safety when the spirit entered her and utter her oracles to those who

9 *Themis: A Study of the Social Origins of Greek Religion,* p. 502.
10 Farnell, *Cults of the Greek States,* p. 173.

sought advice from her. This device was supported by three legs, hence its name, tripod.[11]

Aeschylus describes the passing of the oracle from the earth goddess, Gê or Gaia, to Apollo in the Pythia's prayer in the opening scene of *The Eumenides:*

> First of all Gods I worship in this prayer
> Earth, the primeval prophet; after her
> Themis, the Wise, who on her mother's throne—
> So runs the tale—sat second; by whose own
> Accepted will, with never strife nor stress,
> Third reigned another earth-born Titaness,
> Phoebê; from whom (for that he bears her name)
> To Phoebus as a birthtide gift it came.[12]

Aeschylus describes the story as taking place peacefully and by consent, but apparently this was cleaned up for classical audiences. Older versions, such as the Homeric hymn to Pythian Apollo, speak of a violent struggle in which the god had "slain with his powerful bow the female Dragon, the huge and monstrous beast"—the serpent Python who guarded the shrine of Gê.[13] Thus we see the heroic nature of Homeric Apollo.

But even earlier, the slaying of the Python was yet another version of the battle of the year-king. As in many hero stories of the period of transition into patriarchy, Apollo does not relinquish the throne to the next contender; thus he breaks the matriarchal cycle, keeping the Delphic oracle for himself. In *The Encircled Serpent,* M. Oldfield Howie notes that historically Apollo superseded Gaia when the Greeks took possession of the country and conquered its earlier inhabitants:

> Perhaps it is this event that is symbolised by the story of the slaying of the Python by Apollo,—the subjugation of the older religion,— henceforward to be regarded as the Evil One,—by the new. .
> . . But although to outward seeming the goddess was conquered, and

---

[11] Flacelière, *Greek Oracles,* p. 38.

[12] Aeschylus, *The Eumenides,* lines 1-8 (Phoebus is one of Apollo's many names).

[13] Flacelière, *Greek Oracles,* pp. 34-35.

her religion, like its guardian, the Python, slain, yet their influence was far from dead, but continued to make itself felt as long as did that of the superseding creed. The skin of the slaughtered Python was used to cover the tripod on which the pythia, who had now nominally become the priestess of Apollo, still sat to continue her functions and reveal the will of the reigning god.[14]

In *The Courage to Create,* Rollo May describes the archaic period as a time when the Greeks were experiencing the anxiety of new possibilities, of expanding outer and inner limits—psychological, political, aesthetic, spiritual. The stability of the family was crumbling; the forms of governing the city-states, the interpretations of the gods, all were in a state of flux. "In such a period of change and growth, *emergence* is often experienced by the individual as *emergency* with all its attendant stress."[15]

May recalls walking through the Greek room of the National Museum in Athens and being struck by the dilated eyes of early statues of Apollo, giving an impression of "great alertness"—which he contrasts with the "relaxed, almost sleepy eyes" of fourth-century classical figures like the Apollo Belvedere (page 18).

These dilated eyes of the archaic Apollo are characteristic of apprehension. They express the anxiety—the excessive awareness, the "looking about" on all sides lest something unknown might happen—that goes with living in a fomenting age.[16]

The shrine of Delphi rose to prominence during the turning point in Greek history. E.R. Dodds explains the importance of Apolline Delphi in this period:

Without Delphi, Greek society could scarcely have endured the tensions to which it was subjected in the Archaic Age. The crushing sense of human ignorance and human insecurity, the dread of divine *phthonos,* the dread of *miasma*—the accumulated burden of these things would have been unendurable without the assurance which such an omniscient divine counsellor could give, the assurance that behind the seeming chaos there was knowledge and purpose. "I know

---

[14] *The Encircled Serpent,* pp. 139-142.
[15] "The Delphic Oracle as Therapist," pp. 113-114.
[16] Ibid., p. 118.

the count of the sand grains and the measures of the sea." Out of his
divine knowledge, Apollo would tell you what to do when you felt
anxious or frightened; he knew the rules of the complicated game
that the gods play with humanity; he was the supreme . . . "Averter
of Evil."[17]

At this time, Apollo differentiated from his brother Dionysus.
While the latter continued to be worshiped as a nature deity, Apollo
lost his chthonic qualities and became more identified with spirit. He
became the god of reason and logic. Form, proportion and the golden
mean were essential if the archaic Greeks were to learn to control the
deep passions and dark powers that they knew so well in nature and
in themselves.[18]

Apollo came to represent truth and beauty, distance and objectivity: He who shoots from afar. He taught the value of abstraction and
self-reflection. Apollo's influence grew in classical times, encom-
passing law, music, poetry, astronomy, mathematics, science,
medicine and philosophy, reaching a peak in his association with
Pythagoras, Socrates and Plato.[19]

Here we find the transition from the old matriarchal to the new patriarchal order all but complete. Apollo reigned as the most Greek of
all the gods throughout the classical period; and Delphi, the navel of
the Earth, became the supreme religious center of Greece.

But what became of the primordial mother goddess? The classical
playwright Aeschylus speaks to this very issue in *The Eumenides,*
the last play in *The Oresteia* trilogy. On the face of it, the play depicts
the trial of Orestes for killing his mother, Clytemnestra, to avenge the
murder of his father, Agamemnon. But in fact, the purpose of the
trial is not simply to determine Orestes' guilt or innocence. It also
seeks to establish whether matriarchal or patriarchal law will prevail.

Classical scholar Gilbert Murray describes matriarchal law thus:

> Whenever kindred blood is shed, the intolerable stain falls first and
> most directly on the face of Mother Earth. It pollutes her, and she
> sends up her punishments from below, blight and barrenness and

---

17 *The Greeks and the Irrational,* p. 75.
18 Rollo May, The Courage to Create, pp. 114-115.
19 Graves, *Greek Myths,* vol. 1, p. 82; Kerényi, *Apollo,* p. 51.

plague, just as to the innocent in normal times she sends life and fruitfulness. Thus we see that blessing as well as cursing lies in the power of the Chthonian people, the dead, the Erinyes, and collectively of Mother Earth. They who send can also withhold.

The law that "The doer shall suffer" is a natural law like the maturing of seed, or the return of spring; most of all like the growth and diminishing every year of the power of the Sun. For that diminishing is really a punishment due to the *Hubris* which the Sun committed when at his height. . . . The rule that blood calls for blood, that *Hubris* goes before a fall, or that sin brings punishment, stands as an unbroken natural law, and the Erinyes are its especial guardians. . . .

The law of . . . the Erinyes neither understands nor forgives. It simply operates.[20]

In *The Eumenides,* the Furies sing:

> Up, let us tread the dance, and wind—
> The hour is come!—our shuddering spell.
> Show how this Band apportions well
> Their fated burdens to mankind.
> Behold, we are righteous utterly.
> The man whose hand is clean, no wrath
> From us shall follow: down his path
> He goeth from all evil free.

> But whoso slays and hides withal
> His red hand, swift before his eyes
> True witness for the dead we rise:
> We are with him to the end of all.[21]

Aeschylus was writing at the dawn of a new era. For him, Zeus, the father and ruler of heaven, was the founder of a new world and promised escape from this endless chain of ancient blind vengeance. "Zeus who learns and understands is also the Zeus who can forgive the sinner."[22]

---

20 Aeschylus, *The Eumenides,* introduction, pp. vii, ix.
21 Ibid., lines 308-319.
22 Ibid., p. ix.

Here is a brand new idea—redemption through consciousness. In *The Eumenides,* the redemptive God is Apollo himself—the *prophetes dios,* revealer of Zeus.[23]

Athena presides over the trial of Orestes, with Apollo and the Furies as witness for the defense and the prosecution respectively. But it becomes a battle of the sexes replete with name-calling. Apollo charges the Furies, threatening them with expulsion:

> Get ye from my door!
> Darken this visionary dome no more!
> Quick, lest ye meet that snake of bitter wing
> That leaps a-sudden from my golden string,
> And in your agony spew forth again
>    The black froth that ye have sucked from tortured men!
> This floor shall be no harbor to your feet. . . .
> Some reeking lion's lair
> Were your fit dwelling, not this cloistered Hall
> Of Mercy, which your foulness chokes withal.
>    Out, ye wild goats unherded! Out, ye drove
> Accursed, that god nor devil dares to love![24]

The Furies' accusation is that it is Apollo who has masterminded Orestes' act and who is guilty of this most heinous of all sins against Mother Earth, matricide:

> These be the deeds ye do, ye Gods of the younger race:
>    Ye break the Law at your will; your high throne drips with gore,
> The foot is wet and the head. There is blood in the Holy Place!
> The Heart of Earth uplifteth its foulness in all men's face
>    Clean nevermore, nevermore![25]

And so fly the accusations until the judges cast their stones. The stones are cast equally, but one judgment still remains. Athena votes to free Orestes, thus pledging her support to the new patriarchal order. Her rationale:

> For, lo, no mother bare me: I approve
> In all—save only that I know not love—

---

[23] Ibid., lines 18-19.
[24] Ibid., lines 179-185, 194-198.
[25] Ibid., lines 162-166.

The man's way. Flesh and spirit I am His
Who gave me life.[26]

The Erinyes respond thus to the judgment against them:

That this should fall on me,
Me of the ancient way,
The faithful of heart! To be
Unclean, abominable
In the darkness where I dwell,
    And my honor shorn away!
My breath is as a fire flung far and wide,
And a strange anguish stabbeth at my side.
Hear thou my wrath, O Mother, Night, mine own,
Hear what these young false-handed gods have wrought!
Mine immemorial honour is overthrown,
    And I am naught![27]

Athena appeases the Erinyes by promising them a home in Athens
and respect from her citizens. The Erinyes become the Eumenides.
And the play ends on this note:

Outpour ye the Chalice of Peace where the torches are blending
    In Pallas the place it is found and the task it is done.
The Law that is Fate and the Father the All-Comprehending
    Are here met together as one.[28]

Reading this play from a modern vantage point, one can see in its
lysis the optimism of the Golden Age, not to mention a pretty piece
of patriarchal propaganda. We know that the Erinyes were not so
easily assuaged, remembering their threat:

Shall not mine injury turn
And crush this people? Shall not poison rain
Upon them, even the poison of this pain
    Wherewith my heart doth burn?[29]

---

[26] Ibid., lines 737-740.
[27] Ibid., lines 863-874.
[28] Ibid., lines 1044-1047.
[29] Ibid., lines 816-819.

No doubt Apollo had to emancipate himself and wrest his own power from the Great Mother. He had to claim a separate identity without which he could never have developed into the highly differentiated form he attained in classical Greece. But as his power became more entrenched, his primordial fear of the matriarchy hardened into patriarchal misogyny. He forgot his roots in the mother goddess, and eventually denied any value to motherhood at all.

Melanie Klein, in "Some Reflections on the Oresteia," asserts:

> If we consider Apollo's attitude, there are indications that his complete obedience to Zeus is bound up with hatred of women and with his inverted Oedipus complex. . . . His hatred of women also enters into his command that Orestes should kill his mother, and into the persistence with which he persecutes Cassandra, whatever her failing towards him might have been. The fact that he is promiscuous is in no contradiction to his inverted Oedipus complex. By contrast, he praises Athena who has hardly any feminine attributes and is completely identified with her father.[30]

Speaking of Athena, Apollo says:

> No nursling of the darkness of the womb,
> But such a flower of life as goddess ne'er
> Hath borne.[31]

Apollo's misogyny reflects the larger Manichaean tradition which asserts that "matter, evil, darkness, and female are interchangeable concepts."[32] With such an attitude, it is no wonder that Apollo had such bad luck in his numerous amours; Cassandra was only one of many.

Even the Pythia resisted him. The following is Virgil's description of Apollo's revelation to the Sybil in *The Aeneid:*

> The god! Behold! The god! . . .
> As she spoke these words before the entranceway,

---

[30] *Envy and Gratitude,* p. 285. The boy with an inverted Oedipus complex experiences negative affect toward his mother and strong attachment to his father. Since the oedipal battle thus becomes too dangerous, the boy defends against his aggressiveness by identifying with the feminine.

[31] Aeschylus, *The Eumenides,* lines 670-672.

[32] Hillman, *Myth of Analysis,* p. 219.

Her face and her color suddenly changed;
Her hair flew into disarray; her breast heaved,
And her wild heart was swollen with frenzy. She seemed to grow
In size and made sounds not mortal. She breathed in
The now approaching god. . . .
But the prophetess had not yet submitted to dread Apollo;
She ran for frenzy about the cave as if she could
Shake off the great god from her breast. But all the more
He tormented her raving countenance, overpowering her fierce heart,
Yanking and tugging the reins.[33]

Similarly, in Pär Lagerkvist's novel, *The Sybil*, the prophetess bemoans her ambiguous fate:

I shake my fist at him who treated me so, who used me in this way, in his pit, his oracle pit—used me as his passive instrument—raped my body and soul, possessed me with his frightful spirit, his delirium, his so-called inspiration, filled me with his hot breath, his alien fire, and my body with his lusting, fertilizing ray. . . . Who chose me to be his sacrifice, to be possessed by him, to foam at the mouth for god. . . . Who has exploited me all my life; who stole from me all true happiness, all human happiness; who bereft me of all that others may enjoy—all that gives them security and peace . . . . all, all—and gave me nothing in return, nothing but himself. Himself. Who is in me still, filling me with his presence, his unrest, never giving me peace because he himself is not peace; never forsaking me. Never forsaking me!
I shake my fist at him, my impotent fist![34]

If this is the sentiment of the Pythia—a woman chosen for and well-schooled in the maintenance of the integrity of her vessel—then we can better understand Cassandra's resistance to Apollo. She was a victim of her times, the era that gave rise to a sado-masochistic pattern of male-female relationships and a collective negative mother complex, both of which continue to affect us.

The transition to patriarchy had undermined the ancient matriarchal values, shaking Cassandra's feminine identity to its very roots. Even

---

[33] Kerényi, *Apollo*, pp. 16-18, quoting Virgil's *Aeneid*.
[34] *The Sybil*, pp. 137-138.

the source of mantic authority, traditionally the domain of the mother goddess,[35] was now in the hands of Apollo.

## Personal Dynamics

As we have seen, Cassandra's relationship to the archetypal mother was on shaky ground. Her relationship to her personal mother, Hecuba, was also deeply afflicted. Cassandra was among the youngest of Hecuba's nineteen children. Graves gives us this version of Apollo bestowing the gift of prophecy, illustrating how she was neglected:

At her birthday feast, celebrated in the sanctuary of Thymbraean Apollo, Cassandra tired of playing and fell asleep in a corner, while her parents, who had drunk too much wine, staggered home without her. When Hecuba returned to the temple, she found the sacred serpents licking the child's ear and screamed for terror. The serpents at once disappeared into a pile of laurel boughs, but from then on Cassandra possessed the gift of prophecy.[36]

This story shows not only her parents' neglect but also her mother's own panic in the face of the dark numen. Yet other references portray Hecuba as the dark feminine herself. Thus we get a picture of Hecuba as very split.

On the one hand, she is ideal queen of Troy, apparently committed to the new patrilineal succession through Priam.[37] Christa Wolf shows Hecuba reprimanding Cassandra for crying in public because tears cloud one's reasoning powers.[38] Hecuba clearly embraced the principles of Apollo, who was even known to be the father of two of her nineteen children (Troilus and Hector).

But her other side is revealed later in the story. After the war, Odysseus won Hecuba as his prize. But she uttered such hideous curses against him and the Greeks for their barbarity and infidelity that they put her to death. "Her spirit took the shape of one of those

---

[35] See Erich Neumann, *The Great Mother,* pp. 292-296.

[36] *Greek Myths,* vol. 2, p. 263.

[37] Wolf, *Cassandra,* p. 293; see also Marion Zimmer Bradley, *Firebrand.*

[38] *Cassandra,* p. 37.

fearful black bitches that follow Hecate, leaped into the sea and swam away towards the Hellespont."[39]

Cassandra's experience of her mother was full of double messages. "Hecuba, my mother, knew me when I was young and ceased to concern herself with me. 'This child does not need me,' she said. I admired and hated her for it. Priam, my father, needed me."[40] Thus Cassandra is totally abandoned when she does not sufficiently mirror her mother's need to be needed. But later, when she seeks out maternal containment from her father, she is warned: " 'You, Cassandra,' Hecuba said to me, 'make sure that you do not burrow too deep into your father's soul.' "[41]

Cassandra did not heed this advice.

> Neither will I forget the father I loved more than anyone else when I was a child. . . . I, Father's favorite and interested in politics like none of my numerous siblings, was allowed to sit . . . in Priam's lap, my hand in the crook of his shoulder.[42]

But their love was largely idealized. Cassandra expressed an awareness of this fact: "The intimacy between us was based, as is so often the case between men and women, on the fact that I knew him and he did not know me. He knew his ideal of me; that was supposed to hold still."[43] But it didn't. Whenever she disagreed with him he would turn on her. And as things got worse for the Trojans, Priam's weak and confused but intractable, even cruel, nature emerged more and more.

When finally Cassandra uttered her dire predictions about the Trojan defeat, Priam imprisoned her in the citadel, with directions to the wardress to keep him informed of her prophecies. Thus by controlling her, he could keep his fear and distrust of her dark femininity at bay. And while publicly disavowing and condemning her as a mad woman, he could secretly use her gift.

---

[39] Graves, *Greek Myths,* vol. 2, p. 341.

[40] Wolf, *Cassandra,* p. 12.

[41] Ibid., p. 41.

[42] Ibid., p. 13.

[43] Ibid., p. 50.

Priam betrayed not only Cassandra but also another daughter, the beautiful Polyxena, whom he exchanged to the Greeks for Hector's body. Thus the Trojans were reduced to the brutish level of the Bronze Age Greeks, with Priam committing an act not too different from Agamemnon's sacrifice of Iphigenia at Aulis.

The similarity between Priam and Agamemnon does not stop here. With an ironic twist, Christa Wolf spins the story that in a chance first meeting in the marketplace, Agamemnon is struck with Cassandra's resemblance to his daughter.[44] Later he wins Cassandra as a spoil of war. When he takes her back home with him to Mycenae, he exhorts his wife, Clytemnestra, to treat Cassandra well: "Tend her with all gentleness. . . ./ She is the prize and chosen flower of Ilion's treasuries,/ Set by the soldiers' gift to follow me."[45]

In his naiveté and hubris as the conquering hero returned, Agamemnon expects his wife to accept the girl. He does not realize that he is adding insult to injury. To Clytemnestra, Cassandra is a rival, not the long-lost daughter Agamemnon is atoning for. Standing over their bloody bodies with the goddess's double ax in hand, Clytemnestra speaks:

> By the perfect vengeance of my child
> By [Hec]Ate and the powers of hell
> (To whom I sacrificed this man), . . .
>
>    Here lies the degrader of this woman:
> Petted and fooled by every gilded girl at Troy.
> And here *she* lies, his battle booty,
> Clairvoyant, concubine,
> Faithful fortuneteller, bedder down— . . .
> A well rewarded pair. . . .
> Yes, here he lies, and here is she:
> The swan who warbled out her swansong, his beloved,
> Leading such a dainty morsel to my bed.[46]

Thus for Cassandra the oedipal triangle is reconstellated. Melanie Klein points out that the hostility between Cassandra and Clytemnes-

---

44 Ibid., p. 103.

45 Aeschylus, *The Agamemnon,* lines 954-959.

46 Aeschylus, *The Orestes Plays,* p. 87.

tra illustrates an important feature of the daughter-mother relationship—the rivalry between two women for sexual gratification by the
same man:

> Because Cassandra had been Agamemnon's lover, she could also feel
> like a daughter who had actually succeeded in taking away the father
> from the mother and therefore expects punishment from her. It is
> part of the Oedipus situation that the mother responds—or is felt to
> respond—with hatred to the oedipal desires of the daughter.[47]

Here the expected retaliation by the mother proves fatal. In the
manner of the hysteric, Cassandra cannot negotiate the oedipal situation. But this failure has its roots in the pre-oedipal experience, in the
symbiosis and separation phases of development. Cassandra's
mother was unable to provide an adequate holding environment for
her child, who needed more than she could give. The mother could
neither fill the child's needs nor tolerate the negative affects which
ensued. To allay overwhelming anxiety, the child would have had to
remain in a symbiotic, merged state, existing only to mirror her
mother's needs.

To avoid being swallowed up in such a symbiotic merger or being
attacked or abandoned if she declared her own needs, the child turned
to her father. The father, also starved for the mother's love, wel-
comed his daughter's attention and affection. In her, he could find a
love object and soul-mate over whom he had power. The girl is once
more in the position of having to mirror a parent's needs. Her own
needs are for oral gratification, not the genital sexual activities of an
adult. She identifies with the father as a mother-surrogate. This further splits her from an embodied feminine ego and even more
strongly elicits the mother's rage and envy.

Poor Cassandra, abandoned by Hecuba, betrayed by Priam, de-
luded by Agamemnon, murdered by Clytemnestra, disbelieved by all;
hoping for the best, seeing the worst; always looking for a safe
haven, a good mother, even in Apollo. But Apollo wanted more than
just filial affection in return for his gift. And she refused to give herself to him sexually. Although she was chosen, she was unable to
fulfill her Sybilline potential. She could not receive him as a

---

[47] *Envy and Gratitude,* pp. 284-285.

woman—genitally from below—like the Pythia seated on the tripod, being filled with his divine inspiration. She could only receive him like a child, orally, when he spat into her mouth, cursing her.

No matter which way she turned, Cassandra was neglected, attacked or asked to give up her identity in order to mirror another. Because of her medial nature, she was used as a projection field, but she lacked the ego boundaries that would have allowed her to disidentify from what others wanted her to be.

Christa Wolf describes Cassandra's conflict:

There *was* a fight going on inside me. I saw that all right. Two adversaries had chosen the dead landscape of my soul as their battlefield and were engaged in a life-and-death struggle. Only madness stood between me and the intolerable pain which these two would otherwise have inflicted on me.[48]

What is this battle that rages within Cassandra? It is the archetypal battle of the sexes, whose lines are clearly drawn by two of Cassandra's parental figures:

Agamemnon: 'Tis graceless when a woman strives to lead.
Clytemnestra: When a great conqueror yields, 'tis grace indeed.[49]

And if the lines of battle are drawn in *The Agamemnon,* then, as we have seen, in *The Eumenides* the war rages on between Apollo and the Furies. Athena acted both as judge and member of the jury. She exonerated Orestes and thereby legitimized matricide and established patriarchal supremacy.

No wonder the goddess was no help to Cassandra when she sought protection in her temple during the massacre of Troy. In fact, Cassandra was raped by Ajax in the shadow of Athena's statue. Cassandra could have found no safe maternal container here. Athena was herself too much a daughter of the patriarchy, betraying her sex and, like Apollo, her own roots in the snake goddess. She appeased the Furies with a promise of respect, packing them off to a subterranean shrine, but in fact they may as well have been banished. Meanwhile

---

[48] *Cassandra,* p. 60.
[49] Aeschylus, *The Agamemnon,* lines 940-941.

Meanwhile Apollo, the golden boy, emerged unscathed. And he has basically remained unchallenged up to the present.

But let us not forget the Erinyes' threat: "My Law, if it be broke,/ Shall come again in wrath to haunt this folk."[50] Through the ages, the dark goddess has made attempts to assert herself but the patriarchy has managed to repress her each time. So she has stayed underground, hiding either in the shadows of esoteric religion (Kabbalism, alchemy, Wicca) or in the unconscious, breaking through in the form of psychopathologies such as hysteria and what we now call borderline conditions.

We have viewed Cassandra as a mythological figure and a tragic character. We have explored her psychodynamics, the personal and collective wounds that led to her demise. Lest we think that Cassandra's life came to a dead end on that sorrowful day at Mycenae, let us look at how the mythological pattern has survived in the Cassandra complex throughout the ages and still struggles in the feminine psyche today.

Goddesses of Fate.
(Coin of Diocletian, ca. 300 A.D.)

---

[50] Aeschylus, *The Eumenides,* lines 719-720.

# 3

# Hysteria—The Wandering Womb

Cassandra personifies the archetypal conflict between matriarchal and patriarchal values, both vying for supremacy and with no eros to connect them. Hysteria has long been a manifestation of this psychic split. This chapter provides an historical frame and a prelude to our later discussion of the meaning of hysteria today.

As we have seen, Cassandra's tragedy was her inability to fulfill her destiny as Pythia, sacred vessel for divine prophecy. Psychologically, her negative mother complex subverted the development of an ego grounded in the matrix of the feminine Self. Because of this, Cassandra suffered from a lack of feminine ego containment—in effect, she had no womb.

There is in fact a four-thousand-year-old tradition of viewing hysteria as a disease of the womb. The uterine causation theory reaches back to the beginning of recorded time and has been adhered to throughout history with few exceptions. Since both the recording of history and the diagnosis of hysteria are patriarchal phenomena, we have no way of knowing if such a syndrome even existed in matriarchal times.

Written medical documents from Egypt date back to 1900 B.C. The oldest of these, the Kahun Papyrus, deals specifically with the subject of hysteria, which it describes as a disease of women caused by " 'starvation' of the uterus or by its upward dislocation with a consequent crowding of the other organs."[1] The physician's efforts were directed toward nourishing the hungry organ or returning it to its original home.

> The parts were fumigated with precious and sweet-smelling substances to attract the womb; or evil-tasting and foul-smelling substances were ingested or inhaled to repel the organ and drive it away

---

[1] Veith, *Hysteria,* p. 3.

from the upper part of the body where it was thought to have wandered.[2]

The Greeks retained this association and even gave the disorder its name, after the word *hystera* meaning womb.[3] Here is Plato's graphic description:

> What is called the matrix or womb, a living creature within them with a desire for child-bearing, if it be left long unfruitful beyond the due season, is vexed and aggrieved, and wandering throughout the body and blocking the channels of the breath, by forbidding respiration brings the sufferer to extreme distress and causes all manner of disorders.[4]

In antiquity, hysteria was viewed as a tangible, concrete and logical reaction to an organic imbalance of the body resulting from the uterus being out of rhythm with its own nature. Sexual factors, especially abstinence, were considered to be the predominant cause, and sexual indulgence the treatment of choice.

When Christianity took hold, natural instincts such as sexuality often became associated with evil. Sexual abstinence became a virtue, not the cause of a disease. And certainly sexual indulgence was not to be prescribed as a therapeutic measure.[5] In the Middle Ages, disease in general became a manifestation of innate evil and the result of original sin.[6] The hysteric was no longer seen as a sick human being in emotional and physical distress.

> Hysteria ceased to be a disease—it became the visible token of bewitchment and thus fell within the domain of the Church, the Inquisition, and even the temporal powers, since penalties were inflicted by the lay arm.[7]

For centuries countless innocent people were accused, tortured and murdered as witches. Hysterics fit well into this atmosphere—

---

2 Ibid.

3 Ibid., p. ix.

4 Hillman, *Myth of Analysis*, p. 253, quoting Plato's *Timaeus*, 91c.

5 Veith, *Hysteria*, p. 43.

6 Ibid., p. 49.

7 Ibid., p. 56.

both as the victims upon whom a spell had been cast and as those who admitted to being witches, trying to "surpass each other in enlarging upon the raptures of the imaginary joys of the flesh in response to their inquisitors' eager and cruel persuasion."[8]

According to the *Malleus Maleficarum*, the cooperation of devil and witch took place in indulgence "in every kind of carnal lust . . . and all manner of filthy delights."[9] Devils were thought to collect human semen which they would inject into the bodies of human beings who would then act as vehicles for the devils' nefarious purposes. Thus, once again, the hysteric acts as the vessel for the god, this time Satan.

Of course, women were the devil's chief target.

> The tears of a woman are a deception, for they may spring from true grief or they may be a snare. When a woman thinks alone she thinks evil! . . . An imperfect animal; she always deceives . . . [She is] more carnal than a man as is clear from her many carnal abominations. . . . Envy and jealousy are women's chief emotions. . . . Their memories are weak, intelligence wanting, and affections and passions inordinate.[10]

Medical historian Ilza Veith traces these ideas to St. Augustine, whose writings were the chief sources of reference and confirmation for the Inquisitors. "They were undoubtedly exalted by a sense of righteousness, feeling secure in using their literal translation of Augustine's words in carrying out the will of the Lord."[11]

Even while the Church and so-called religious healers were burning hysterics as witches, there continued to be secular physicians who carried on the Greco-Roman practices of diagnosis and treatment. Swiss physician Paracelsus, while rejecting the wandering womb theory, listed hysteria as among the diseases which "deprive man of his reason" and proposed that "the cause is that the matter on

---

[8] Ibid., p. 59.

[9] Ibid., p. 61, quoting Kramer and Sprenger, *The Malleus Maleficarum*, trans. Montague Summers (London: Pushkin Press, 1951), p. 21.

[10] Ibid., pp. 63-64, quoting *Malleus Maleficarum*, p. 43.

[11] Ibid., p. 59.

which the womb is internally nourished and kept alive destroys itself, like wine returning into vinegar."[12]

The sixteenth-century writer Rabelais speaks to this in rather more ribald terms:

> Plato, you will recall, was at a loss as to where to class them [women], whether among the reasoning animals or the brute beasts. For Nature has placed in their bodies, in a secret and intestinal place, a certain animal or member which is not in man, in which are engendered, frequently, certain humors, brackish, nitrous, boracious, acrid, mordant, shooting, and bitterly tickling, by the painful prickling and wriggling of which—for this member is extremely nervous and sensitive—the entire feminine body is shaken, all the senses ravished, all the passions carried to a point of repletion, and all thought thrown into confusion. To such a degree that, if Nature had not rouged their foreheads with a tint of shame, you would see them running the streets like mad women, in a more frightful manner than the ... Bacchic Thyades on the day of their Bacchanalia ever did; and this, for the reason that this terrible animal I am telling you about is so very intimately associated with all the principal parts of the body, as anatomy teaches us.
>
> I call it an "animal," in accordance with the doctrine of the Academics. . . . For if movement, as Aristotle says, is a sure sign of something animate, and if all that moves of itself is to be called an animal, then, Plato was right, when he called this thing an animal, having noted in it those movements commonly accompanying suffocation, precipitation, corrugation, and indignation, movements sometimes so violent that the woman is thereby deprived of all other senses and power of motion, as though she had suffered heart-failure, syncope, epilepsy, apoplexy, or something very like death.[13]

In 1603, Edward Jorden wrote the first English work on hysteria, based on his experience as an expert medical witness in a witchcraft trial when he diagnosed the victim of an accused witch as an hysteric and attributed her afflictions to natural causes:

---

[12] Ibid., p. 105, quoting Paracelsus, *On the Diseases that Deprive Man of His Reason* (Basel, 1567).

[13] Ibid., pp. 107-108, quoting Rabelais, *Pantagruel,* in *The Portable Rabelais,* trans. Samuel Putnam (New York: Viking Press, 1946), pp. 477-478.

This disease is called by diverse names amongst our Authors, *Passio Hysteria, Suffocatio, Praefocatio,* and *Strangulatus uteri, Caducus matricis,* etc. In English the Mother, or the Suffocation of the Mother, because most commonly it takes them with choaking in the throat: and it is *an affect of the Mother or wombe wherein the principal parts of the bodie by consent do suffer diversely according to the diversitie of the causes and diseases wherewith the matrix is offended.*[14]

This choking sensation was known as the *globus hystericus.* The other parts of the body suffer "by consent," which occurs via a "sympathetic interaction" from the afflicted womb with a secondary organ, making the latter a "partaker of grief," or through some noxious substance such as "vapors."[15] The term vapors in fact originated at this time and later became synonymous with hysteria, but is also reminiscent of the gasses thought to emanate from the chasm at Delphi—the vapors from the womb of Mother Earth.

James Hillman calls Jorden's book a

watershed, separating the ancient superstition called possession from the modern superstition called hysteria. . . . The witch is now a poor patient—not evil, but sick. The psychiatric protection from evil does not do away with the evil but merely shifts it into secular terms. The misogyny does not change; it appears in a new form.[16]

Hillman further quotes medical historian Esther Fischer-Homberger: "Where hysteria is diagnosed, misogyny is not far away."[17]

By the seventeenth century the seat of the affliction had moved from the uterus to the brain. Hysteria became a disease of the mind and a behavioral, psychological disorder. But it never lost its sexual connotation. William Harvey still charged that the cause of hysteria,

---

[14] Ibid., pp. 121-122, quoting Jorden, *A Briefe Discourse of a Disease called the Suffocation of the Mother* (London: John Windet, 1603), chapter 2, p. 5 (italics in original).

[15] Ibid.

[16] *Myth of Analysis,* p. 254.

[17] Ibid., quoting Fischer-Homberger, "Hysterie und Misogynie" (dissertation, University of Zurich, 1969).

which he called *furor uterinus,* was "over-abstinence from sexual intercourse when the passions are strong."[18]

In the eighteenth century, the psychiatric innovator Philippe Pinel, who introduced the "moral treatment" for insanity, described hysteria as one of the "genital neuroses of women."[19] Robert Carter continued the development along psychodynamic lines, paving the way for Freud's theory of sexual repression. Thus abstinence evolved into repression as the primary etiological factor in hysteria:

> An emotion, which is strongly felt by great numbers of people, but whose natural manifestations are constantly repressed in compliance with the usages of society, will be the one whose morbid effects are most frequently witnessed. This anticipation is abundantly borne out by facts; the sexual passion in women being that which most accurately fulfills the prescribed conditions, and whose injurious influence upon the organism is most common and familiar. Next after it in power, may be placed those emotions of a permanent character, which are usually concealed, because disgraceful or unamiable, as hatred or envy; after them others equally permanent, such as grief or care, but which, not being discreditable, are not so liable to be repressed. . . .
>
> While the advance of civilization and the ever-increasing complications of social intercourse tend to call forth new feelings, and by their means to throw amativeness somewhat into the shade, as one powerful emotion among many others; still its absolute intensity is in no way lessened, and from the modern necessity for its entire concealment, it is likely to produce hysteria in a larger number of the women subject to its influence, than it would do if the state of society permitted its free expression. It may, therefore, be inferred, as a matter of reasoning, that the sexual emotions are those most concerned in the production of the disease.[20]

---

18 Veith, *Hysteria,* p. 130, quoting William Harvey, *On Parturition; in the Works of William Harvey, M.D.,* trans. Robert Willis (London: Sydenham Society, 1847), p. 54.

19 Ibid., p. 179, quoting Philippe Pinel, *Nosographie philosophique ou la méthode de l'analyse appliqué à la médicine* (5th ed.; Paris: J. A. Brosson, 1813), p. 285.

20 Ibid., pp. 201-202, quoting Robert Carter, *On the Pathology and Treatment of Hysteria* (London: John Churchill, 1853), pp. 34-35.

While Carter's formulations display a profound understanding of the sociological and psychological plight of the nineteenth-century woman, he does not sound as sympathetic when he describes the hysteric as allying "selfishness and deceptivity" and using her affliction to get attention for secondary gain.[21]

This moralizing attitude was consistent with a wave of misogyny during what can be viewed as the epidemic of hysteria that arose in the nineteenth century. A German contemporary of Carter's named Wilhelm Griesinger insisted that "all local diseases of the uterus, ovaries, and vagina are likely to be followed by hysteria, which then may gradually progress into insanity."[22] He attributed to hysterics an "inclination to deceive and to lie, traits of decided envy, smaller or greater nastiness."[23]

Jules Falret, French psychiatrist at the Salpêtrière Hospital, reveals these same sentiments:

> These patients are veritable actresses; they do not know of a greater pleasure than to deceive . . . all those with whom they come in touch. The hysterics who exaggerate their convulsive movement . . . make an equal travesty and exaggeration of the movements of their soul, their ideas, and their acts. . . . In one word, the life of the hysteric is nothing but one perpetual falsehood; they effect the airs of piety and devotion and let themselves be taken for saints while at the same time secretly abandoning themselves to the most shameful actions; and at home, before their husbands and children, making the most violent scenes in which they employ the coarsest and often most obscene language and give themselves up to the most disorderly actions.[24]

In the eighteenth century another influence arose which was in turn to have a great effect on the treatment of hysteria. The Viennese

---

[21] Ibid., p. 203, quoting Carter.

[22] Ibid., p. 197, quoting Wilhelm Griesinger, *Mental Pathology and Therapeutics,* trans. C. L. Robertson and J. Rutherford (London: New Sydenham Society, 1867), p. 201.

[23] Hillman, *Myth of Analysis,* p. 256, quoting Griesinger.

[24] Veith, *Hysteria,* p. 211, quoting essay by Falret, "Folie raisonnante ou folie morale," in *Etudes cliniques sur les maladies mentales et nerveuses* (Paris: Librairie Baillière et Fils, 1890), p. 502.

physician Franz Anton Mesmer theorized that disease was caused by an imbalance of the "universal fluid" that flowed between man and the cosmos, and that cure could be effected by bringing the patient into contact with the source of the fluid by means of a magnet or the human hand. Mesmer's theory of animal magnetism did not win favor from the scientific community of his time. His practices smacked of charlatanry and theatrics, attracting criticism similar to that of hysterics themselves. The following is a description of a typical seance:

> Mesmer made his appearance with the accompaniment of soft mournful music. He slowly passed among his patients, draped in a lavender-colored silken robe or suit, fixing his eyes upon each in turn and touching them with his hands or with a long magnetized iron wand. . . . Beguiled by this impressive ritual, the participants, predominantly women, fell into a somnolent trance or mesmeric sleep, from which they awoke refreshed and healed. The suggestion that the state of well-being may have been sexual gratification that was perhaps not entirely elicited by astral influence has often been raised.[25]

Mesmer's techniques presumably had their roots in esoteric tradition which, as we shall see, would have done justice to the hysteric and accounted for much of his success in treatment. And even though Mesmer withdrew into obscurity after being discredited by the medical community, the doctrine of animal magnetism managed to survive.

In France, one of Mesmer's students, the Marquis de Pysegur, believed that in the state of magnetic or somnambulist sleep patients displayed a complete change in personality and acquired the power of clairvoyance, which was not present in the waking state.[26] Thus we see the recognition of mediumship during an altered state of consciousness, reminiscent of the Pythian oracle of antiquity.

In Scotland, James Braid, at first a complete skeptic who then became profoundly interested in the subject, first introduced the terms neuro-hypnotism and hypnosis, showing that these phenomena are

---

[25] Ibid., pp. 222-223.
[26] Ibid., p. 224.

"induced solely by an impression made on the nervous centers" and are not due to a "mystical universal fluid."[27]

Braid's study was a major influence on one of the most famous proponents of hypnosis as a treatment for hysteria, Jean-Martin Charcot, who established his fame as a neurologist and teacher at the Salpêtrière Hospital. In his later years, his chief concern was the study of the neuroses, hysteria and hypnotism. It was his over-confidence in hypnosis that cost him most of the respect he had won early on. Even though he is known for his observations of hysterical contagion and the role of suggestion in creating certain symptoms of hysteria, what caused his undoing was his assumption that the *grande paroxisme* of his hysterical patients under hypnosis was a typical characteristic of the disease. In fact, his assistants who induced the trance state had, unbeknownst to Charcot, implanted suggestions in the minds of the patients to perform according to their chief's expectations.[28]

Another major contribution by Charcot was the significance he attributed to psychological trauma in the production of hysterical attacks. He treated his patients by removing them from the psychopathogenic environment:

It is necessary to separate both children and adults from their father and their mother, whose influence, as experience teaches, is particularly pernicious.

Experience shows repeatedly, though it is not always easy to understand the reason, that it is the mothers whose influence is so deleterious, who will hear no argument, and will only yield in general to the last extremity.[29]

Charcot's trauma theory, along with Carter's formulations regarding repression, laid the groundwork for the conceptualization of the complex. Charcot's pupil, Pierre Janet, continued this develop-

---

[27] Ibid., pp. 225-226, quoting James Braid, *Neurypnology; Or the Rationale of Nervous Sleep, Considered in Relation with Animal Magnetism* (London: J. Churchill, 1843).

[28] Ibid., p. 239.

[29] Ibid., pp. 235-236 quoting Charcot, "Isolation in the Treatment of Hysteria," in *Clinical Lectures on Diseases of the Nervous System,* trans. Thomas Savill (London: New Sydenham Society, 1889), p. 210.

ment when he observed that the hysterical manifestations of an individual patient were highly repetitious and predictable, and that their automatic behavior was organized around certain emotional reactions and ideas. The idée fixe was subconscious and "one could not treat the hysterical behavior before having reached those deep layers of thought within which the fixed idea was concealed."[30]

Janet's weakness was his theory of etiology. He dismissed the theory of uterine causation as well as the belief in the hypereroticism of hysterical patients:

> After having accused hystericals of all crimes of witchcraft, and having reproached them with cohabiting every Saturday with the devil, disguised as a he-goat, people have long preserved a vague remembrance of these superstitions, and have maintained that these patients had an eminently erotic disposition.[31]

In a humane attempt to free the disease from misogynous attacks, he dropped a crucial thread to its symbolic meaning. As I noted earlier, Janet expressed a poetic appreciation for the word hysteria, even though he felt that it had become etymologically meaningless.

Janet's devotion to the word was not shared by all of Charcot's students. The famous neurologist Joseph Babinski coined what he thought was a new name for the illness—*pithiatisme*. This combined the Greek words *peitho,* meaning "I persuade," and *iatos,* meaning curable. Babinski believed that the most important factor involved in both the diagnosis and treatment of the hysteric was her suggestibility, which then enabled a cure by persuasion, that is, the doctor's suggestion.[32]

Whether or not Babinski was aware of the Pythian connotation of his neologism, he came very close to an actual association between Cassandra and hysteria. It is interesting to note that, according to Larousse, when Apollo breathed into Cassandra's mouth, "though he left her with the power of foretelling the future, he took from her the

---

[30] Ibid., p. 252, quoting Janet, *The Mental State of Hystericals,* p. 412.

[31] Ibid., p. 250, quoting Janet, p. 215.

[32] Ibid., p. 255, quoting J. Babinski and J. Froment, *Hysteria or Pithiatism and Reflex Nervous Disorders in the Neurology of War* (London: University of London Press, 1918).

power of persuasion so that from then onwards no one would believe what Cassandra predicted."[33] No wonder then that for the hysteric, as with Cassandra, the ability to persuade rests with the Apollonian authority figure and, in the analytic situation, with the analyst.

Charcot's most famous pupil was Sigmund Freud, whose interest in hysteria gave him his starting point in the development of psychoanalysis. In a collaborative effort with Joseph Breuer entitled *Studies in Hysteria*, Freud set down his earliest formulations of the treatment he called catharsis. This involved tracing hysterical symptoms back to traumatic events in the patient's life and removing these symptoms by recreating the original situation under hypnosis.[34]

Subsequently, Freud's work was devoted to the transition from catharsis to psychoanalysis. He found that he was able to explore unconscious and repressed memories without altering the patient's mental state. The use of hypnosis and suggestion was replaced by free association and the analysis of dreams, resistance and transference.

As recently as 1946, Freud himself observed that in associating hysteria with sexuality, he "was going back to the very beginnings of medicine and reviving a thought of Plato's."[35] Earlier, when he wrote that sexuality is not purely mental but also has a somatic aspect which through chemical processes produces "particular, though at present unknown, substances,"[36] he could not have been fully aware of the historical context of such ideas. Not only was he reiterating Galen and the theories of humors and vapors, but he was also predicting the field of endocrinology which may hold the key to bridging the gap between mind and body.

---

[33] *Larousse,* p. 118.
[34] Veith, *Hysteria,* p. 261.
[35] Ibid., p. 265, quoting Freud, *An Autobiographical Study,* trans. James Strachey (London: Hogarth Press, 1946), p. 41.
[36] Ibid., quoting Freud, p. 42.

# 4

# Beyond the Patriarchal Perspective

Freud's treatment of hysteria is still practiced today, even though its prevalence has supposedly decreased. Ilza Veith explains why she thinks hysteria has become an infrequent illness:

> In this century behavior that includes "kicking about" and "waving the arms and legs" is met with distaste and lack of sympathy and is tolerated at best only among shrieking mobs of teenaged girls in response to their current idols. . . . Unacceptable today would be the fainting ladies of the Victorian period, partly because they would altogether fail to evoke any sympathetic response in their social environment. . . . Thus hysteria has become subjectively unrewarding. The helpful concern that was shown for hysterical women throughout the ages up to early in this century has given way to uncomprehending indifference. . . .
>
> Freud's studies on hysteria, instead of endowing this illness with greater significance, actually divested it of most of the mystical importance it had held for more than two millennia. . . . If, as has been stated, hysteria is primarily a means of achieving ego-satisfaction, this lack of attention could easily account for the nearly total disappearance of the illness. Thus, it may not be too paradoxical to state that it was the intensified understanding of the cause of hysteria by leading psychiatrists during this century that contributed to the near-disappearance of the disease. The newly gained insight into therapy finds its application in the severe psychoneuroses in general within which the potential hysterics of today are presumably included.[1]

We may not see seizures and convulsions anymore, but to overlook hysteria or view it as obsolete is to ignore a well-defined clinical syndrome.

Veith based her view that hysteria has disappeared on the fact that it was eliminated from the diagnostic manual of the American Psychiatric Association in 1952 and was replaced by the term

---

[1] *Hysteria,* pp. 273-274.

"conversion symptom." But in 1968, three years after the publication of Veith's book, the revised manual (DSM II) carried descriptions of both hysterical neurosis and hysterical personality:

> *Hysterical Neurosis:* This neurosis is characterized by an involuntary psychogenic loss or disorder of function. Symptoms characteristically begin and end suddenly in emotionally charged situations and are symbolic of the underlying conflicts. Often they can be modified by suggestion alone.[2]

> *Hysterical Personality* (Histrionic Personality Disorder): These behavior patterns are characterized by excitability, emotional instability, over-reactivity, and self-dramatization. This self-dramatization is always attention-seeking and often seductive, whether or not the patient is aware of its purpose. These personalities are also immature, self-centered, often vain, and usually dependent on others.[3]

Otto Kernberg further differentiates hysterical neurosis and hysterical (infantile, histrionic) personality disorder in several ways. The latter, which he classifies as a borderline condition, presents poor object relations and issues which are largely pre-oedipal. In the neurotic, oedipal issues predominate and, in relationships other than sexual ones, there is a depth and maturity not found in the personality disorder. While both are sexually seductive, the neurotic tends to be frigid, while the other is less inhibited and tends toward "polymorphous perverse" sexuality.[4]

Kernberg characterizes hysterics in general as emotionally labile, displaying warm exaggerated feelings along with childlike thinking and reasoning abilities. They tend to be extraverted and exhibitionistic, provocative and pseudo-hypersexual. Their behavior is clinging, dependent and overinvolved, and they are often submissive and masochistic in relationships.

David Shapiro describes hysterical cognition as impressionistic, marked by global emotional reactions. The hysteric is deficient in

---

[2] *Diagnostic and Statistical Manual of Mental Disorders* (DSM II), p. 39.

[3] Ibid., p. 43. DSM III has now subsumed diagnoses of hysteria under the categories of "Somatoform and Dissociative Neuroses" and "Histrionic Personality Disorder."

[4] "Psychoanalytic Psychotherapy with Borderline and Narcissistic Patients."

factual knowledge, being romantic and sentimental rather than objective, and has little capacity for intellectual concentration. She gets her answers through hunches or inspiration. While usually rather mild mannered she is subject to emotional outbursts, abrupt discharges of affect that subside quickly and are experienced later as something that has passed through her without her real participation, as if an alien force had taken possession of her.[5]

Shapiro treats the subject in a Freudian mode, reductively and negativistically, focusing on defensive repression, inferior cognition and infantile behavior. He does not see any constructive potential or meaning in the hysterical symptoms. Although his tone is somewhat derogatory, his observations are nonetheless poignant and relevant. In fact, they accord quite closely with Jung's description of hysteria as an affliction of the extraverted feeling type, whose judgments are largely dictated by custom and tradition and whose thinking function is infantile, archaic and negative.[6] One might hope for a more constructive approach to hysteria in Jung, but from the condescending tone of his description it sounds as though he too were caught by the misogyny of his times and perhaps his own negative mother complex.

James Hillman explains this "reductivity," which is so uncharacteristic of Jung, even antithetical to the principles of analytical psychology. Jung derived the idea of an *abaissement du niveau mental,* a lowering of the level of consciousness, from Janet, who associated it with a "psychological insufficiency" leading to hysteria. Even though Janet made a valiant attempt to free hysteria from misogyny, he continued to regard it as an inferiority of functioning and one that was especially feminine.[7]

Jung carried on this tradition by referring to the inferior part of the function as an *abaissement* in which there is *participation mystique*—identification—with the surroundings and the collective unconscious. Hence, writes Hillman,

> in Jungian analysis as now practiced in general, the *abaissement* and inferiority are associated with the red end of the archetypal spec-

---

[5] *Neurotic Styles,* chapter 4.

[6] *Psychological Types,* CW 6, pars. 597-600.

[7] *Myth of Analysis,* p. 252.

trum—with emotion and with communal and physical life—and the inferior aspect of a function is considered inferior also in a value sense.[8]

More relevant to the Cassandra complex, Hillman points out that it is Apollo himself who is the source of the reductive medical view of hysteria. Referring to Apollo's statement in *The Eumenides* that "the mother is no parent of that which is called her child. . . . There can be a father without any mother," Hillman asserts:

> The Apollonic fantasy of reproduction and female inferiority recurs faithfully in the Western scientific tradition. We call it "Apollonic" because . . . [it] evokes the purified objectivity and the scientific clarity of masculine consciousness. The Apollonic view of the feminine appears to be inherent in the same structure of consciousness as the methods by which the fantasy is supposedly proven. . . . We should expect to find Apollo especially in the language of medical science, since Apollo is the father of Asclepius, God of medicine.[9]

Thus we can trace Apollo's legacy to modern medicine, both his gift of scientific methodology and the curse of misogyny.

As long as hysteria continues to be seen only as an illness, there is no hope of finding a constructive meaning in its symptomatology. For example, we know that frigidity is a common symptom of hysteria and is actually used to make a differential diagnosis. Even the term is condescending and smacks of male reference, viewing the phenomenon only as a deficit rather than as a valid need for some. There are many women who have good psychological reasons for being unable to give themselves over to desire and orgasm.

Ilza Veith believes that hysteria has "adapted its symptoms to the ideas and mores current in each society; yet its predispositions and its basic features have remained more or less unchanged."[10] The consistencies are the assumption that hysteria is exclusively a disease of women and the sexual imagery that has surrounded it. As Veith

---

[8] Ibid.
[9] Ibid., p. 225.
[10] *Hysteria,* p. viii.

remarks, "Throughout the tangled skein of its history runs the scarlet thread of sexuality."[11]

Hysterical symptoms express unconsciously not only what has been personally repressed but also what has been collectively unacknowledged. Robert Carter was aware of this fact back in the eighteenth century.[12] So it makes sense that modern symptomatology would not be the same as in Freud's day. As Neil Micklem writes:

> Hysteria has not been changed by the times; rather it has itself been in the service of that unseen mover behind the times, bringing the change of pattern and alternation in style . . . and appearing as a compensation to the prevailing conscious attitude.[13]

In the most general sense, throughout the patriarchal era hysteria has compensated for prevailing masculine values and, conversely, expressed or acted out unconscious feminine values. At any time, one need only look at the hysterical symptomatology to see what particular unconscious or repressed values seek integration into the mainstream of culture.

From our modern perspective, for instance, we can see that Victorian hysterics were expressing the sexual repression of their times. Freud interpreted the motor phenomena of hysterical attacks—the seizures and convulsions, the screaming and crying—as an acting out of the affects appropriate to infantile memories. But Freud's interpretation may be a Victorian patronization and denial of what also could be the movements (tonic and clonic contractions) and sounds of an adult woman having an uninhibited orgasm.

Sexual repression, per se, is no longer the specific problem of our time. But hysteria is still prevalent and continues to be found primarily in women. So what repressed feminine values is the hysteric currently carrying?

I believe that mediality is the predominant unconscious value that is being compensated by the hysteric today. Consider Toni Wolff's picture of the medial woman:

---

11 Ibid.
12 See above, p. 42.
13 "On Hysteria: The Mythical Syndrome," p. 153.

The medial woman is immersed in the psychic atmosphere of her environment and the spirit of her period, but above all in the collective (impersonal) unconscious. The unconscious, once it is constellated and can become conscious, exerts an effect. The medial woman is overcome by this effect, she is absorbed and moulded by it and sometimes she represents it herself. She must for instance express or act what is "in the air," what the environment cannot or will not admit, but what is nevertheless a part of it. It is mostly the dark aspect of a situation or of a predominant idea, and she thus activates what is negative and dangerous. In this way she becomes the carrier of evil, but that she does, is nevertheless exclusively her personal problem. As the contents involved are unconscious, she lacks the necessary faculty of discrimination to perceive and the language to express them adequately. The overwhelming force of the collective unconscious sweeps through the ego of the medial woman and weakens it . . . .

By its nature the collective unconscious is not limited to the person concerned—further reason why the medial woman identifies herself and others with archetypal contents. But to deal with the collective unconscious demands a solid ego consciousness and an adequate adaptation to reality. As a rule the medial woman disposes of neither and consequently she will create confusion in the same measure as she herself is confused. Conscious and unconscious, I and you, personal and impersonal psychic contents remain undifferentiated. . . . As objective psychic contents in herself and in others are not understood, or are taken personally, she experiences a destiny not her own as though it were her own and loses herself in ideas which do not belong to her. Instead of being a mediatrix, she is only a means and becomes the first victim of her own nature.[14]

This sounds like a description not only of the hysteric but of Cassandra as well. Indeed, Christa Wolf has her speak of her medial experience as follows:

---

[14] Toni Wolff, "Structural Forms of the Feminine Psyche," pp. 9-10. The medial woman is one of four types described by Wolff; the other three are the mother, the hetaira and the amazon. Wolff's paper is not easily available outside of Jung Institute libraries, but a summary of her model appears in Donald Lee Williams, *Border Crossings* (Toronto: Inner City Books, 1981), pp. 119-122.

Time stood still, I would not wish that on anyone. And the cold of
the grave. The ultimate estrangement from myself and from every-
one. That is how it seemed. Until finally the dreadful torment took
the form of a voice; forced its way out of me, through me, dismem-
bering me as it went; and set itself free. A whistling little voice,
whistling at the end of its rope, that makes my blood run cold and
my hair stand on end. Which as it swells, grows louder and more
hideous, sets all my members to wriggling and rattling and hurling
about. But the voice does not care. It floats above me, free, and
shrieks, shrieks, shrieks.[15]

Certainly Aeschylus's description of Cassandra in *The Agamemnon*—"driven to the point of madness by the impact of the prophetic
fit"[16]—is not unlike Freud's description of "the painful affect, crying, screaming, raving" of the hysteric.[17] Likewise, the seventeenth-
century account, by physician William Harvey, of "mental aberra-
tions, the delirium, the melancholy, the paroxysms of frenzy, as if
the affected person were under the dominion of spells,"[18] is similar
to the following description of the Pythia in the throes of prophetic
trance:

The boldest colours would scarcely suffice to paint the convulsions
with which she was soon after seized. We saw her bosom heave, her
countenance change, and all her limbs agitated by involuntary mo-
tions; but she uttered only plaintive cries and deep groans. At length,
with eyes sparkling, foaming mouth, and hair erect . . . she tore the
fillet from her head, and amid the most dreadful howlings pronounced
a few words.[19]

Classical scholar E.R. Dodds claims that the god used the Pythia's
voice "exactly as the so-called 'control' does in modern spirit mediumship."[20]

---

[15] *Cassandra*, p. 59.

[16] Flacelière, *Greek Oracles*, p. 36.

[17] Hillman, *Myth of Analysis*, p. 253.

[18] Veith, *Hysteria*, p. 130, quoting Harvey, *On Parturition*, p. 543.

[19] Howie, *Encircled Serpent*, p. 145.

[20] *The Greeks and the Irrational*, p. 70.

Psychiatrist Jan Ehrenwald clearly articulates the link between the Pythia, the trance medium, the witch and the hysteric, pointing out that common to them all is

> the production of secondary personalities and states of apparent possession, of specific symptoms of conversion hysteria, of what Renaissance physicians called melancholia or what the witch hunters of Salem dubbed the suffocating mother.
>
> Thus, viewed in the perspective of modern clinical psychiatry, there is an unbroken line of continuity from the fits and convulsions of the nuns of Loudun or Louviers, the witches of Salem, Mesmer's somnambulists, and Charcot's hysterics to some of the more dramatic manifestations of the mediumistic trance.[21]

The trance itself, notes Ehrenwald, has been a recurrent feature in all historical periods:

> It is found in Egypt and the Far East, as well as in the Sybils and Pythias of Greco-Roman antiquity; it was among the well-nigh obligatory credentials of the Hebrew prophets from Amos and Hosea to Jeremiah and Isaiah. It is part of the folklore of most preliterate peoples from the voodoo priests and priestesses of Haiti and other witch societies of the West Indies to the medicine men and shamans of South America, Siberia, and Central Africa. The religious raptures and ecstacies or some other altered states of consciousness, sometimes amounting to trance, are among the characteristics of many Catholic mystics and saints. Some of them, including St. Theresa of Avila and Joan of Arc, seem often to have teetered on the borderline between witchcraft and saintliness.[22]

The suggestibility and receptivity of the hysteric has always been well known, but her positive medial potential has rarely been recognized. Toni Wolff beautifully describes the constructive function of the medial woman as a carrier of collective values and interpreter of the Zeitgeist:

> The present contains within itself the past and the future. The lucidity of consciousness rests upon dark, unconscious seeds out of which have grown or will grow the objective cultural values. It is this un-

---

[21] *The E.S.P. Experience: A Psychiatric Validation,* p. 35.
[22] Ibid.

conscious background which is perceived by the *medial* structural form.

. . . If she possesses the faculty of discrimination, the feeling or the understanding for the specific values and the limits of the conscious and the unconscious, of the personal and the impersonal, of what belongs to the ego and what to the environment, then her faculty to let herself be moulded by the objective psychic contents will enable her to exert a positive cultural influence. . . . In that case, she consecrates herself to the service of a new, maybe yet concealed, spirit of her age.[23]

For this to happen, writes Wolff, it is imperative that the medial woman become conscious and acquire discrimination,

so as to become a mediatrix instead of a mere medium. Instead of identifying herself and others with collective unconscious contents— quite unrelated to reality—she ought to appreciate her medial faculty as an instrument and receptacle for the reception of these contents.[24]

Wolff points out an interesting fact, that the first medium in recent times appeared in 1848, the same year as the beginning of female emancipation and the publication of the *Communist Manifesto* by Marx and Engels. Some believe that this period was the dawn of the Aquarian Age, which would indicate a vital role for the medial woman in the new aeon.

But in order to function positively, the medial woman must have a strong ego vessel, one which knows its boundaries, can discriminate the personal from the transpersonal and can communicate. Her ego must also be permeable, so that she can receive the collective impressions which it is her task to mediate. Thus the traditional patriarchal model of ego structure does not suffice.

Jan Ehrenwald observes that "more than half a  century after the advent of relativistic physics and quantum mechanics, our theories of personality are still steeped in the classical Judeo-Christian or Aristotelian tradition."[25] The personality is conceived of as an impenetrable fortress—a self-contained, closed and isolated system—operating

---

[23] Wolff, "Structural Forms of the Feminine Psyche," pp. 8-10.

[24] Ibid., p. 10.

[25] Ehrenwald, *E.S.P. Experience*, p. 205.

in a universe extended in Euclidean space and prerelativistic time, ruled by Newtonian laws of mechanics and subject to Aristotelian laws of cause and effect. Ehrenwald states that "the rejection and repudiation of the telepathic factor by the growing child's ego has become mandatory in our culture."[26] Instead, he calls for an open, transpersonal model of personality, one that is pervious to psi phenomena (telepathy, clairvoyance, precognition).

Ehrenwald names the new model a personality without walls. While his observations are exciting and poignant, to my mind he goes a step too far. His concept of a boundaryless personality overlooks the need for individual containment. Perhaps a more fitting image is an ego which has boundaries that operate like a semipermeable placental membrane. Such a model provides for both openness and integrity. The new ego must be able to hold onto awareness while in a trance state and tolerate what the patriarchy calls an *abaissement du niveau mental.*

Erich Neumann recognizes that such a lowering of the level of consciousness is crucial for mediumship:

> The female psyche is in far greater degree dependent on the productivity of the unconscious, which is closely bound up with what we accordingly designate as the matriarchal consciousness.
>
> But precisely this matriarchal consciousness which rests in large part on man's *participation mystique* with his environment, and in which the human psyche and the extrahuman world are still largely undivided, forms the foundation of the magical-mantic power of the human personality.[27]

But the hysteric lacks the feminine ego vessel needed to mediate this level of awareness. Her patriarchal, animus-identified ego is in her head, not grounded in her emotional/imaginal/body awareness.

David Shapiro describes the hysteric as "without that sense of substance" that one needs in order to resist "impressive transient influences."[28] He is referring to emotional substance, but the need is also physical. The ego of the medial woman must be embedded in

---

26 Ibid., p. 25.

27 *Great Mother,* p. 293.

28 *Neurotic Styles,* p. 121.

this feminine matrix, not to resist collective influences but rather to relate to them consciously.

When Freud said that woman's "impaired genital" was "ground for inferiority,"[29] he was not far off but, as so often, he was concretizing a symbolic truth. He was referring to her "stunted penis," but it is not maleness that is stunted in the hysteric. The male organ in her psyche, the animus, is actually hypertrophied. What is impaired is her female organ, her ego vessel, her womb. This is the real ground for her so-called inferiority. And why not?—when the feminine has been systematically attacked, criticized, devalued, raped, murdered, burned, pricked, fumigated, surgically excised, patronized, mesmerized, and repressed for thousands of years.

The medial woman's ego needs to be flexible, embodied and syntonic with the feminine Self. This is her psychological womb, her center, her omphalos.[30] And when her womb wanders, she is lost.

We now understand the symbolic meaning of the term "wandering womb." Psychologically, it refers to an ego which is not grounded in the emotional, imaginal matrix of the Self.

We have examined the collective factors which undermine the development of such a Self-syntonic ego. We have also seen that hysterical symptomatology is the unconscious expression of repressed feminine values and compensates for prevailing patriarchal values; further, mediality is a central feminine value being carried by the hysteric today.

Let us now look at the experience of some modern Cassandra women.

---

[29] Hillman, *Myth of Analysis,* p. 241, quoting Freud, "The Dissolution of the Oedipus Complex" (1924), Standard Edition, vol. XIX, p. 178.
[30] See below, pp. 91-93.

# Part Two
# Cassandra Now

Venus of Willendorf.
(Limestone, paleolithic, Austria; Naturhistorisches Museum, Vienna)

# 1

# Dark Visions

Central to a discussion of the psychology of the Cassandra woman is Jung's notion of the morbid complex in the hysteric:

> The complex has an abnormal autonomy in hysteria and a tendency to an active separate existence, which reduces and replaces the constellating power of the ego-complex. In this way a new morbid personality is gradually created, the inclinations, judgments, and resolutions of which move only in the direction of the will to be ill. This second personality devours what is left of the normal ego and forces it into the role of a secondary (oppressed) complex.[1]

A complex develops when the ego is unable to contain and consciously relate to, and thus integrate, some unconscious content. In other words, the ego cannot embody an archetype which is seeking expression. The unconscious content then accrues substance—in the form of related affects, images, memory traces and expectations—around its core, like a crystal that precipitates out of a solution.

What then is the unconscious content which forms the core of the morbid complex? Jung describes it in terms of the extraverted feeling type, whose inferior thinking function

> reaches the surface in the form of obsessive ideas which are invariably of a negative and depreciatory character. . . . The most hideous thoughts fasten on the very objects most valued by their feelings.[2]

The complex takes hold when the personality gets swallowed up by "a succession of contradictory feeling states."[3]

While this formulation rings true phenomenologically, Jung's conclusions about the typology of the hysteric do not fully explain the content of the complex. Nor do they correspond to my own ob-

---

[1] "Association, Dream, and Hysterical Symptom," *Experimental Researches,* CW 2, par. 861.
[2] C.G. Jung, *Psychological Types,* CW 6, par. 600.
[3] Ibid.

servations. For example, the Cassandra woman with her Apollonian animus-ego often has a well-developed thinking capacity, even though it may break down in the face of the morbid complex. And why would a woman whose primary function is feeling be so easily overwhelmed by ambiguity?

Perhaps more cogent than Jung's remarks is the view of Mary Williams, a Jungian analyst who describes the core problem of the hysteric as the negative mother complex—"the experience of the terrible, destroying, devouring mother, that is, the 'dark' aspect of the maiden. In hysterics, this is postulated as being split off and forming a morbid complex which persecutes the ego."[4]

The archetypal core of the morbid complex is therefore the dark goddess; and the obsessive, negative, depreciatory and hideous thoughts described by Jung may be none other than the cyclic, concretistic attributes of the Great Mother in her vengeful, death-dealing aspect. No wonder the Cassandra woman experiences the morbid complex as an attack by the Furies.

Of course, another attribute of the dark goddess is mediality. While the natural superior function of the hysteric is intuition, her essential mediality is not cultivated or even sanctioned by the patriarchy. If anything, her medial nature tends to be exploited or scapegoated. She learns early on to hide it or use it to shape-shift. Her ego is neither strong nor permeable enough to utilize her natural gift.

As we have seen, the Cassandra woman develops a pseudo-ego informed by Apollonian values, what Jung in his description of the hysteric calls "a caricature of the normal"[5] and Williams describes as "an ego ideal which is based on the 'traditional' picture of the good and virtuous woman."[6] This leaves her dark mediality in the shadow, locked within the morbid complex, remaining primitive and undifferentiated, as are all unconscious contents which have no access to the light of day. Hysteria then is the anxiety response of the inadequate ego, unable to contain and process an influx from the unconscious.

---

[4] "A Study of Hysteria in Women," p. 187.

[5] Ibid., p. 178

[6] Ibid.

This psychopathology is exacerbated by the hysteric's afflicted relationship with her personal mother, who tends to be a narcissistic, animus-possessed woman with little connection to her own femininity. She is unable to provide a holding environment for her daughter's needs, which the mother experiences as overwhelming demands. How many mothers of hysterical women were able to sublimate their maternal anxieties in Dr. Spock? What a boost to the mother's animus if the baby could be weaned by three months, walking by nine months and toilet-trained at a year and a half!

Meanwhile there is no positive symbiotic bond, no healthy sense of embodied self constituted in the infant. The child develops the impression that life cannot be lived on her terms, only on her mother's. The child's reality is not believed. She gains her identity only through conforming to her mother's expectations. In a way, the child becomes mother to her own unmothered mother, who needs constant mirroring from and merger with her daughter and spoils enviously when she doesn't get it.

The child's field of consciousness is always projected into the environment; her locus of concern remains external. She carefully watches for cues to how she should behave, for how much of her the other will tolerate, developing a precocious sensitivity to others' needs. As Melanie Klein writes:

> There are babies who refrain from biting the breast, who even wean themselves at an age of about four or five months . . . . Such restraint, I think, indicates that . . . the infant feels that the mother has been injured and emptied by his greedy sucking or biting and therefore in his mind he contains the mother or her breast in an injured state. . . . I would suggest that this complaining injured object is part of the super-ego.
>
> The relation to this injured and loved object includes not only guilt but also compassion, and is the fundamental source of all sympathy with others and consideration for them. In the Trilogy this aspect of the super-ego is represented by the unhappy Cassandra. . . .
>
> Cassandra as a super-ego predicts ill to come and warns that punishment will follow and grief arise.[7]

---

[7] "Some Reflections on 'The Oresteia,' " *Envy and Gratitude,* p. 293.

I believe that while the child may feel rudimentary guilt and compassion, this precocious superego does not indicate the formation of the so-called depressive position.[8] It simply leaves the infant with an injured maternal object. What may seem like normal depression is actually hopeless despair and apathetic withdrawal. The baby's healthy scream fades into a whine. The good object remains only an unmediated potential.

It is no wonder that the child turns to the masculine for nurturance. Even though the father of the hysteric tends to be weak and passive, unable to psychologically penetrate his narcissistic wife, the child idealizes the masculine. She identifies with the idealized father, or, perhaps more correctly, with the mother's Apollonian animus. In effect, there is no mother, no ego-based, feminine identity. The only feminine aspect allowed to surface is the medial, through which the hypertrophied masculine element—the mother's animus, internalized by the daughter—seeks expression. The ego is in the service of the animus, which actually operates more like a narcissistic character structure, demanding positive mirroring at all times. The woman's ego is reduced to playing anima to her own animus.

In the myth, Cassandra refused to consummate her union with Apollo. In the psyche of the Cassandra woman, this aborted *coniunctio* manifests as a severe split, with the Apollonian animus on one side and the hysterical Cassandra shadow on the other. When she is operating out of her animus she can ride the wave of its power, but underneath she feels empty and unfulfilled in spite of her accomplishments. She may be very talented, but is unable to truly claim her gift. Her abilities, largely co-opted by her Apollonian animus, cannot be fully developed but remain superficial because they are not connected to the deeper feminine Self.

One of her gifts is a kind of intuitive insight. This animus-informed intuition has a clear, light, airy quality which has a universal, archetypal ring to it, but resonates strangely with those who hear it.

---

[8] This is the phase of ego integration in which the infant recognizes a whole object, i.e., that both the good and bad breasts are parts of the same mother. It feels loss and guilt—that it has lost the loved object through its own destructiveness. (See Hannah Segal, *Introduction to the Work of Melanie Klein*, pp. 68-70.)

This is because the intuition is ungrounded, not embodied in personal experience. It does not come from the depths wherein lie the dark visions, like Cassandra's prophecies, which the woman herself is terrified to see, let alone speak of in the light of day. The dark medial intuition stays in the shadow, closely akin to the negative pole of the feminine Self. It remains unmediated by the ego which colludes with Apollo. He in turn eschews and rejects the whole bloody, emotional, "Fury-ous" mess.

The shadow may emerge for several reasons: when the Apollonian animus/ego-ideal fails; or on the occasion of an *abaissement* due to illness, exhaustion, etc.; or when the ego is overwhelmed by the dark visions or intense negative affects of the morbid complex. The woman is bereft of the benefit of the Apollonian animus which could help her to focus, understand and articulate her experience. She also loses all sense of embodied ego which could give her some perspective. Possessed by the complex, she sees only the horror. The shadows loom larger than life. She feels attacked not only from the outside world but also from within, especially from the body in the form of somatic, often gynecological, complaints. Normal aches and pains are built up into fatal diseases in her mind. The woman falls prey to all sorts of paranoid ideations which may contain a grain of truth but cannot be reality tested.

What the Cassandra woman sees here is something dark and painful that may not be apparent on the surface of things or that objective facts do not corroborate. She may envision a negative or unexpected outcome; or something which would be difficult to deal with; or a truth which others, especially authority figures, would not accept. In her frightened ego-less state, the Cassandra woman may blurt out what she sees, perhaps with the unconscious hope that others might be able to make some sense of it. But to them her words sound meaningless, disconnected and blown out of all proportion. No wonder she is not believed. She cannot even afford to believe herself; her ego cannot accept what her shadow knows.

Without benefit of Apollo's enlightening clarity, her visions remain dark and chaotic. Whatever potential might be here for deep feminine wisdom is lost—to all.

Serpent and egg mandala with an unusual five-part
outer circle of eyes and wings.
(From C.G. Jung, "A Study in the Process of Individuation," *The
Archetypes and the Collective Unconscious,* CW 9i, p. 347)

# 2

# Healing the Wounds

The therapeutic process for the Cassandra woman involves healing the split between the shadow and the Apollonian animus, thereby promoting the longed-for *coniunctio*. The woman can then claim her gift and fulfill her destiny, so that what she sees can be believed, especially by herself.

This process is double-edged. On the one hand, the ego is developed, strong yet permeable enough to integrate the woman's dark medial aspect. On the other hand, the hypertrophied, narcissistic, Apollonian animus is mortified and reshaped as a positive aspect of the personality.

In the last line of his early paper called "Association, Dream, and Hysterical Symptom," Jung cryptically concludes that the treatment of hysteria involves "introducing some new complex that liberates the ego from domination by the complex of the illness."[1] I posit that this "new complex" is none other than the transformed feminine ego, and that the therapeutic tool through which it is introduced is the transference.

In fact, the crucial factor in treating hysteria may be the transference. This is no new idea. After all, transference theory was originally derived from the psychoanalytic treatment of hysteria and then generalized to other psychopathologies. Jungian analyst Alex Quenk goes so far as to suggest that a patient's readiness to develop a transference may even justify a diagnosis of hysteria.

Quenk follows Jung in viewing hysteria in terms of typology; he sees it as a result of extreme extraverted feeling *and* intuition. He attributes hysterical suggestibility to a lack of introverted judgment:

> It is not surprising that the extreme extrovert would develop a transference, especially since [she] directs [her] energy onto the object and

---

[1] *Experimental Researches,* CW 2, par. 862.

the responses of the person-object provide the evaluative judgment of the extreme extravert's well-being.[2]

Quenk outlines three stages of the transference in the extravert: Will I be loved? Dare I get angry? Dare I love?[3]

While these formulations are apt, to my mind they are too simplistic. There are factors other than typology involved in the development of the hysterical transference. For example, the hysteric's suggestibility is also due to her permeable medial nature. The proclivity to develop a transference reflects the tendency to concretize her need for containment. Likewise, what appear to be extraversion and inferior introverted thinking are, in large part, a lack of interiority due to inadequate ego boundaries.

We know that the Cassandra woman's animus-identified ego cannot contain, and is split off from, the medial shadow, which remains locked within the morbid complex until she can develop an ego to accommodate it. This development is effected by means of a therapeutic regression, within the transferential field, to the pre-separatio stage of maternal symbiosis where the primary fault and consequent split originated.

Any inadequacy in the symbiotic stage has especially disastrous consequences for the medial type, for whom the first and crucial step in all ego development is identification. Maternal failure at this stage impairs not only the child's ego but also the ego-Self axis, giving rise to a deep sense that her essential being is not acceptable.

A therapeutic regression affords the opportunity to repair the fault. The first step involves the dissolution of the ego's identification with the Apollonian animus and the transfer of the identification onto the analytic field. The analytic container becomes the womb in which the new complex—the Self-syntonic, feminine ego—can gestate. Within this temenos, a strongly dependent transference is allowed to grow. The woman can have a healthy experience of projective identification, which repairs the primary fault at the symbiotic level and eventually paves the way for mature medial functioning.

---

[2] "Hysteria: A Dynamic and Clinical Entity."
[3] Ibid.

As she works through the vicissitudes of the transference, culminating in separation, the woman internalizes the boundaries of the analytic container. These boundaries provide a template for the growth of a strong embodied ego that behaves more like a semipermeable membrane than a closed system and can tolerate an *abaissement* without losing consciousness. The woman's ego can function as the medial tool it was meant to be, receiving and processing data both from the outside and from within, via kinesthetic, emotional and imaginal impressions. The results are a highly differentiated empathic capacity, a deep sense of inner authority and a trust in her mediality. Here is a woman who believes what she sees.

Likewise, the disidentification of the ego from the Apollonian animus gets her out of her head and into her body, so that the animus can help her relate to what is, instead of how things should be. Rather than tying up her energy in his own narcissistic defenses, the animus then functions as a bridge to the feminine Self, lighting the way to and from her shadowy depths, so that the ego can perceive the truths from this dark place. He helps her to discriminate between personal and collective unconscious contents, to understand the meaning of what she sees; he enables her to stand her ground and communicate what she knows.

Thus the therapeutic regression to the pre-separatio level affords the opportunity to heal the personal psyche. But the value of the regression does not end there. The healing process also involves the archetypal realm.

While traditional psychoanalytic theory states that hysteria is caused by a fixation at the oedipal stage of development, my formulation places the cause at a pre-oedipal level, with the oedipal disturbances as sequelae. This is not an original idea. Many post-Freudians, including Jung, disagreed with the master on this issue.

In *Symbols of Transformation,* Jung takes issue with Freud's theory that hysteria results from the fear and repression of oedipal desires. While he agrees that Freud's incest theory accurately describes the infantile sexual fantasies that accompany the regression of libido characteristic of the personal unconscious of hysterical patients, Jung feels that Freud's theory does not go far enough.

The last act of the drama consists in a return to the mother's body. This is usually effected not through the natural channels but through the mouth, through being devoured and swallowed, thereby giving rise to an even more infantile theory. . . . The regression goes back to the deeper layer of the nutritive function, which is anterior to sexuality, and there clothes itself in the experiences of infancy. In other words, the sexual language of regression changes, on retreating still further back, into metaphors derived from the nutritive and digestive functions, . . . The so-called Oedipus complex with its famous incest tendency changes at this level into a "Jonah-and-the-Whale" complex, which has any number of variants, for instance the witch who eats children, the wolf, the ogre, the dragon, and so on. Fear of incest turns into fear of being devoured by the mother. The regressing libido apparently desexualizes itself by retreating back step by step to the presexual stage of earliest infancy.[4]

Even more profoundly, Jung goes on to state that the regression

continues right back into the intra-uterine, pre-natal condition and, leaving the sphere of personal psychology altogether, irrupts into the collective psyche where Jonah saw the "mysteries" ("représentations collectives") in the whale's belly. The libido thus reaches a kind of inchoate condition in which . . . it may easily stick fast. But it can also tear itself loose from the maternal embrace and return to the surface with new possibilities of life.

What actually happens in these incest and womb fantasies is that the libido immerses itself in the unconscious, thereby provoking infantile reactions, affects, opinions and attitudes from the personal sphere, but at the same time activating collective images (archetypes) which have a compensatory and curative meaning such as has always pertained to the myth.[5]

It is precisely the work with these archetypal images that promotes the healing of the morbid complex. In *Psychological Types,* Jung writes that the mobilization of the collective unconscious "activates its store of primordial images, thus bringing with it the possibility of a regeneration of attitude on a different basis."[6]

---

[4] *Symbols of Transformation,* CW 5, par. 654.

[5] Ibid, pars. 654-655.

[6] *Psychological Types,* CW 6, par. 600.

What then are the archetypal images relevant to hysteria? Three Jungians—James Hillman, Neil Micklem and Mary Williams—have addressed this question.

Hillman sees Apollo as a central character and the *coniunctio* as a crucial issue in hysteria. He shows how Apollonic consciousness gave rise to theories of female inferiority and establishes the connection between the repression of the feminine and hysteria. Hillman observes that Apollo himself suffered from this feminine repression. He discusses how, as the god developed into his classical form, he identified more and more with patriarchal masculinity, driving the feminine (anima) into projection; hence the many myths in which Apollo chases after various nymphs and maidens. But according to Hillman, "the *seeking* of the *coniunctio,* as Apollo pursuing Daphne, is self-defeating because it hyperactivates the male, driving the psyche into vegetative regression, Daphne into the laurel tree."[7] Thus Hillman recognizes that Apollo creates a split which precludes the possibility of union.

Apollo is not truly seeking *coniunctio.* He only uses the nymphs and maidens and then discards them. He is on a narcissistic power trip, seeking control and mastery of the feminine, lusting simply for conquest.

To remedy the impossibly polarized state created by Apollo, Hillman invokes Dionysus. His rationale is that Dionysian bisexuality offers an androgynous alternative to one-sided Apollonian consciousness. "The *coniunctio* is not an attainment but a given. It is not a goal to be sought but an a priori possibility."[8]

I take issue with Hillman's viewpoint on several counts. First of all, in offering Dionysus as the androgynous reconciling image, he is ignoring the reality of psychic process. There cannot be a third thing without the first two, without the struggle between opposites. *Coniunctio* is not a given, it is hard won. It involves the interaction between polarities, the relationship between two individuals with equal but opposite power.

---

[7] "On Psychological Femininity," *Myth of Analysis,* p. 259.
[8] Ibid.

Perhaps Hillman's intention is to replace the prevailing Apollonian male principle with one which is more related and sympathetic to the feminine, thereby creating an enabling space for *coniunctio*. But the prescription for "tincture of Dionysus" is not the answer to the hysteric's problem. An increased infusion of the masculine would only feed the already hypertrophied animus and again devalue the feminine in the woman's psyche. Before the animus can change, the Cassandra woman must become more grounded in her femininity. Notwithstanding his bisexuality, Dionysus is still a man and, as Hillman presents him, another hero come to rescue the poor hysterical woman. It is a disservice to offer her a deus ex machina. She needs to pull herself out of her inferiority with her own ego, in order finally to meet the masculine, including her animus, on equal terms.

Another problem with Hillman's formulation is a lack of differentiation between two distinct clinical entities, namely the group phenomenon called mass hysteria, which would correctly be associated with Dionysus, and hysterical neurosis which affects the individual and is at its core an issue of afflicted mediality.

Plato clearly expressed the difference. According to E.R. Dodds, he acknowledged Apollo as the patron and inspiration for divine prophetic madness and distinguished between

> Apolline mediumship which aims at knowledge, whether of the future or of the hidden present, and the Dionysiac experience which is pursued either for its own sake or as a means of mental healing, the mantic or mediumistic element being absent or quite subordinate. Mediumship is the rare gift of chosen individuals; Dionysiac experience is essentially collective or congregational . . . and is so far from being a rare gift that it is highly infectious.[9]

To simply replace one archetype with another does neither justice and betrays the archetypal dominant behind Cassandra's plight. She is called by Apollo, not Dionysus. The confusion is understandable in light of the similarities between Dionysus and the archaic Apollo, but Hillman's view denies the unique character of Apollo and the fact that hysterical neurosis is a feminine response to *him*.

---

[9] *The Greeks and the Irrational*, p. 69.

Apollo, from the west pediment of the Temple of Zeus at Olympia.
(Marble, ca. 460 B.C.; Museum, Olympia)

No doubt it is important, now and then, for the healthy, well-adapted woman to blow off steam and connect to her collective feminine roots in a maenadic way. However, for the Cassandra woman with her friable ego the Dionysian experience can be obliterating. Only when she has a strong ego is she able to assimilate the chthonic animus. Then Dionysus can indeed provide her with phallic power, break down rigid outworn structures and promote collective consciousness, and also, as Apollo's dark brother, pave the way for the healthy Apollonian animus to eventually reemerge in the woman's psyche.

Neil Micklem and Mary Williams identify the archetypal motif relevant to hysteria as Demeter-Persephone, described by Williams as "a myth of the disruption of the *participation mystique* of mother-daughter experience, and the consequent 'rape' and 'initiation' of the maiden."[10] Both authors recognize the hysteric as growing up in a family constellation with a forbidding authoritarian mother in the ascendant. The animus-possessed mother prevents the rape by the masculine spirit god; or, as Micklem succinctly states, there is "an interference on the part of the 'mother' (Demeter, womb, or complex) in the relationship between the masculine and the feminine."[11]

But Micklem makes the same mistake as Hillman, by prematurely prescribing more of the masculine. He overlooks the fact that the hysteric is already overidentified with the male element and that what needs to be attended to first is the afflicted relationship to the mother.

As noted in the previous chapter, Mary Williams views the negative mother complex as the core of the hysteric's problem. Describing her therapy of an hysterical patient, she states that

> it was possible to mitigate the terrible mother by bringing out her more positive aspects as the *initiator* . . . [which] seemed to me to form the "new complex" which Jung advocates as necessary to free the ego from the persecution of the morbid complex.[12]

Williams sees the goal of therapy as bridging the gap between maidenhood and womanhood, so that the woman can experience positive initiation and not just destructive rape. Thus she can claim the power of the dark feminine Self, as represented by Persephone, Queen of the Underworld.

What this formulation misses is that the rape/initiation can only be experienced when a woman has had a positive maternal container, which the Cassandra woman has not. The myth of Demeter-Perse-

---

10 "A Study of Hysteria in Women," p. 179.
11 "On Hysteria: The Mythical Syndrome," p. 161.
12 "A Study of Hysteria in Women," p. 187.

phone describes a good mother-daughter relationship—perhaps too good, to the extent that mother and daughter are both reluctant to allow any disruption of their *participation mystique*. I agree that the Demeter-Persephone myth is relevant to hysteria, but not as the starting point of the process. Rather it is a crucial phase in the treatment and the goal of the therapeutic regression.

Neil Micklem puts it well when he states:

> Even as Dionysus is probably not the one archetype of hysteria, so too that of Demeter/Persephone cannot be shown to be the sole basis of the syndrome. Yet somewhere within the Kore, albeit perhaps in association with other Kores—Athene, Artemis, Psyche—would seem to be the pattern of poor relationship, of collapse and the mixture through identification, rather than a coniunctio and the hermaphrodite.[13]

As we will see, all the archetypes Micklem mentions play a role in the transformation process of the Cassandra woman. We can add to his list of Kores Cassandra herself, whose basic problem is indeed "the mixture through identification, rather than a coniunctio." We see in her story, from Troy to Mycenae, an elaboration of the dilemma of the hysteric. But the old myth itself holds no answers to the Cassandra problem, no blueprint for the resolution of the conflict. Cassandra's drama, which took place historically at the dawn of the patriarchal era, was an unmitigated disaster. She was not able to avoid a miserable fate at the hands of the negative mother.

Perhaps some creative resolution is possible as feminine values are reclaimed and the mythology develops in the New Age. My own clinical experience with the modern Cassandra woman in treatment indicates this potential. Perhaps after four thousand years, the tide is turning for the medial woman.

## Phases of Analysis

My observations have led me to conclude that the course of analysis involves a five-phase process of ego and animus development (as opposed to Quenk's three-stage paradigm). Each phase is character-

---

13 "On Hysteria: The Mythical Syndrome," p. 164.

ized by its archetypal dominant, represented by a particular god-
dess/god from the Greek pantheon which manifests in the patient's
psychodynamics and in the transference.

By closely examining both the analysands' material and the countertransference phenomena (my own emotional reactions, images and
kinesthetic perceptions), I have identified these phase-specific domi-
nants. Both diagnostic and prognostic, they offer a blueprint for
healing and reflect the intrapsychic, developmental tasks appropriate
to each phase in the process (see chart opposite). My outline, which
is both theoretical and empirical, represents a work in progress.

My descriptions of the analyst's role may seem idiosyncratic, especially as it relates to the archetypal level of the transference-countertransference. I work largely out of my own medial function and
therefore utilize data gleaned from "feeling through" the archetype
that is operating. Every analyst has his or her own tools and techniques of perception and intervention. My statements concerning the
analyst's role in each phase of the process are not meant to be a prescription for behavior, but rather a guide to understanding the possible clinical manifestations of, and reactions induced by, the archetypes.

Further, while I present these phases sequentially, in actual experience they do not occur in such a neat, linear succession. Rather they
interweave in a manner reminiscent of Kerényi's description of "the
dreamlike unfolding of the drama" at Eleusis where the "primordial
god and goddess undergo endless transformations before they come
together."[14]

Just as the Eleusinian Mysteries evoked the fluid, mythopoeic
quality of worship from a remote matriarchal time, so does the analytic process function for the modern Cassandra woman as she cir-
cumambulates the Self, experiencing the different aspects of the primordial god and goddess. Slowly integrating her experience into ego
consciousness, she repairs the fragmentation and re-members the
original one-ness of the Self. Only then can she encounter the Apollonian animus on equal terms and fulfill her destiny.

---

[14] *Essays on a Science of Mythology,* p. 137.

# PHASES OF ANALYSIS

| ARCHETYPAL DOMINANT | | INTRAPSYCHIC DEVELOPMENTAL TASKS | TRANSFERENCE PHENOMENA |
|---|---|---|---|
| EGO | ANIMUS | | |
| Athena | Zeus | Disidentification of the ego from the patriarchal animus. | Analyst as wise counselor:<br>—establishment of analytic frame<br>—resistances<br>—idealized transference |
| Demeter/Persephone | | Regression to pre-separatio maternal uroborus.<br>Embodiment of rudimentary ego/Self.<br>Dissolution of morbid complex.<br>*(Oral phase)* | Analyst as positive mother:<br>—symbiotic bond/good breast<br>—projective identification *(participation mystique)*; mirroring<br>—transitional object phenomena |
| Hecate | Hades/Dionysus | Separation from maternal uroborus.<br>Integration of dark feminine (especially medial aspect).<br>Emergence of chthonic animus.<br>*(Anal/Oedipal phase)* | Analyst as negative mother:<br>—separation/rapprochement<br>—negative transference/bad breast<br>—depressive position |
| Artemis | Heracles | Consolidation of ego boundaries.<br>Differentiation of ego, shadow and Self.<br>Containment of shadow.<br>Experience of animus as partner.<br>*(Latency phase)* | Analyst as role model:<br>—self-discipline<br>—assertiveness training<br>—confrontation and constructive criticism |
| Themis | Apollo | *Coniunctio* (union of opposites).<br>Recognition of Self (transpersonal superego).<br>Refinement of medial aspect.<br>*(Genital phase)* | Analyst as peer:<br>—creative conflict<br>—symbolic interpretations<br>—termination of analysis |

Birth of Athena from the head of Zeus. Legend has it that she
sprang forth "fully armed, with a mighty shout."
(British Museum, London)

# 3

# Athena

*You have been particularly brilliant in your logic. But to be logical is not to be right—and nothing on God's earth could make it right.*
> —Judge Heywood speaking to the attorney defending Nazi war criminals in *Judgment at Nuremberg*.

In the third of her eight years of analysis, Ellen dreamed:

> I was in the abandoned business district of my home town. It was a depressed, burned-out area, decrepit, decaying, where nothing survives. I was with my mother, father and brother. We were on our way to church to pray. But there was no building—only an empty lot with dirt and pebbles on the ground and steps leading down to a deep pit. It seemed paganistic—maybe ancient Roman. Bells were ringing. I looked up and saw my father ringing them. Then I noticed a black cat's tail and other cats' bodies decapitated all around. It was creepy and I tried not to look. As we approached the steps, a black cat walked by. Then I saw half of a cat's body lying across the steps. I couldn't cross. I just stood screaming, "I hate it!" I was frozen and couldn't move.

This dream is an ominous picture of Ellen's negative mother complex, her spiritual crisis and her deep depression dating back to childhood. Associating to the dream on the subject of religion, Ellen described her inability to find any solace in her family's Judaism.

In the dream, her father calls them to worship. But instead of a church, she finds an empty pit and the dismembered corpses of black cats. The cat is an age-old symbol of the dark feminine, familiar of witches. Ellen's reaction is hysterical horror. She hates cats—"they are slinky and sneaky and give me goose bumps."

Through her identification with her family, Ellen had internalized the religion of her fathers; all that is left of the dark goddess are the corpses of her theriomorphic form—"cut lengthwise, like the way you cut up chickens for soup." The dismemberment of the cats

79

shows how disenfranchised she is from her true worship and how cut off she is from the feminine Self.

Ellen's analytic process involved "work on what has been spoiled"[1] and the resurrection of her life from the wasteland of her parents' world. This dream reflected a breakthrough of insight into her obsessive fantasies of having breast cancer. Until then, her dreams had often been of empty rooms with black walls or of her children being murdered.

Here is another of her early dreams:

> I go to see someone in a mental hospital—a young, dark woman. I want to help her, but she starts to choke me.

The dark young woman is an image of the morbid complex, the split-off shadow. The dream ego feels choked by the shadow. This choking sensation is the *globus hystericus* of which Ellen often complained when she felt overwhelmed by terror, rage or envy. She had reported the same choking sensation in association to the previous dream, when she saw the cats. This is her ego's reaction when confronted with the dark feminine, here in human rather than animal form. The dream-ego wants to help but is attacked. The shadow is too unintegrated, split off; but at least now it is contained, institutionalized, thus offering some hope of treatment and rehabilitation.

This dream illustrates the relationship of ego to shadow at the onset of the process, the Athena phase. Here the ego *looks* healthy; as mentioned in the previous chapter, Jung calls this state a caricature of the normal. The dreamer is able to function only by keeping the morbid shadow locked up, hidden away. As Ellen said, "You want me to have emotions, but I don't want to feel anything. It's better to be under control; at least I'm functioning."

One can see in the dream the labeling and scapegoating of the morbid complex as the identified patient. The dark feminine has no value in the patriarchy and the ego colludes with the Apollonian medical model in diagnosing her, which only adds to her rage. The ego identifies with the animus in splitting off the shadow. Archetyp-

---

[1] See *I Ching*, Hexagram 18.

ally this is Priam, who locked up Cassandra for making predictions he did not want to hear.

Ellen's ego here is functioning like a caricature of clear-eyed Athena, an ego ideal to which Ellen very much aspired. Athena was extraverted, intelligent, active, honest; a father's daughter, born out of Zeus's head. She was much admired by Apollo. But it was Athena who let Cassandra be raped in her temple in the shadow of her statue.

Athena was also the one who banished the Furies to their underground cave. Is it not the Furies driving Ellen's shadow to choke her, thus enacting their threat in *The Eumenides* to haunt with wrath those who break their law?[2]

Another analysand, Sarah, also experienced the morbid complex as an attack by the Furies. She complained of chronic back pain early in her analysis. In a Gestalt exercise, she was able to visualize an image of this pain, namely a great vulture over her shoulder wanting to hurt or kill her. In the process of analysis, as she was able to integrate her shadow into ego consciousness, her back pain subsided.

When she first came to treatment, Sarah, like Ellen, defended against this morbid complex with an Athena-like, animus-identified ego. In fact, she reported a childhood fantasy that she had been born from the family's grandfather clock. Early on she dreamed:

> I see a book entitled *Inner Light,* by Cassandra Castleglove.

On the face of it, this dream indicates that Sarah can find consciousness through the logos endeavors of her Cassandra aspect. But the dream also reveals both Sarah's compensation for her inner darkness and the character structure she has erected to defend against it. A castle is a fortification, an aspect of the patriarchal feudal system. Gloves protect the hands, keep them clean and hide fingerprints, which can establish guilt through personal identity. They also prevent sensation. Years later, Sarah had the following insight: "Cassandra Castleglove guards me. She is clear and right and direct and fearless. She keeps me from going too deep into myself. She is what I hide behind."

---

[2] See above, p. 36.

The Cassandra in this dream is the father's daughter who turned to Priam because she could find no positive maternal container in Hecuba. It is Clytemnestra who finally takes revenge on Cassandra for taking up with the father. Here again the throat is attacked: Clytemnestra cuts off Cassandra's head, a literal image of the mind-body split.

Both Ellen and Sarah looked to their fathers to protect them from the negative mother. Ellen dreamed:

> I was sleeping in my bed. I thought I heard someone in the hall. I called out "Daddy." The hall light dimmed to darkness. I realized I was calling my husband.

As a young woman, when she began to suffer from somatic delusions, Ellen would call her father to assure her that she did not have cancer. When she left her husband and a loveless marriage of security and convenience, she lost a patriarchal defense against the negative mother complex and her cancer phobia got worse.

Similarly, Sarah has a four-year-old oedipal memory of calling her father to carry her to the bathroom at night because she was afraid of "the monsters on the ground." Sarah was in fact terrified of her mother, a strict Episcopalian given to bouts of violent irrationality and hysteria, a woman whose own mother was a self-avowed witch.

As a child, Sarah had little choice but to identify with her father who encouraged his bright little girl's psychological incest insofar as she mirrored his soul. It was not until her adolescence that the destructive nature of their collusion was revealed, when her father informed her of his homosexuality, in a most disturbing and unconscious manner. It was as though her budding pubescence threatened their incestuous union. He attempted to spoil her female sexuality as Apollo spoiled Cassandra's gift when he cursed her. In fact, Sarah's menarche came late and was always accompanied by severe cramps.

The likeness of the Cassandra woman's father to Apollo does not end there. Sarah's father was an academician with a brilliant mind and a refined aesthetic sensibility. She admired and identified with these qualities. But even these fine Apollonian attributes have their shadow: Phoebus, "light and holy," becomes holier than thou; Agyieus, "purifier and healer," becomes obsessive/compulsive; Hyberborean Apollo, ideal and remote, the god of objectivity, perspective, logic and harmony, becomes cold, withdrawn and schizoid. Described by the elders in *The Agamemnon*, "[Apollo] loves not grief nor lendeth ear to it."[3]

Melanie Klein says of this description that Apollo

> is not able to experience compassion and sympathy with suffering . . . [which] reminds one of the people who turn away from any sadness as a defense against feelings of compassion, and make excessive use of denial of depressive feelings.[4]

This is Apollo in his classical form, cut off from his matriarchal roots, projecting darkness and negativity onto the Erinyes, disavowing himself of any need for the feminine but forever chasing after nymphs. Christa Wolf observes:

> "Know thyself," the maxim of the Delphic oracle, is one of Apollo's slogans. . . . [Apollo] is unable to attain the self-knowledge he strives for. The thin regions whither he and his disciples retreat, fearing to be touched. . . are cold. They need cunning little devices to avoid dying of the cold. One of these devices is to develop women as a power resource. In other words, to fit them into their patterns of life and thought. To put it more simply, to exploit them.[5]

This characterization of Apollo describes not only the father of the Cassandra woman but also her inner man. This is a very dangerous animus for a woman who is not grounded in a strong feminine ego. Her power pools in the animus. It does not function as a bridge to the feminine Self. It connects her up and out instead of in and down. Her field of consciousness is projected onto the animus and externalized. Ego and animus collude in a narcissistic defense, so as not to feel pain and inferiority. Everything is larger than life and idealized.

The woman may be articulate and outspoken in her opinions, even compulsively honest, but in an unrelated way and perhaps off the mark. Sarah, for instance, would often tell fabulous, overblown stories, which she herself experienced as running off at the mouth. She

---

[3] Aeschylus, *The Agamemnon*, line 1074.

[4] *Envy and Gratitude*, p. 295.

[5] *Cassandra*, p. 294.

was also prone to grandiose fantasies when the morbid complex was constellated. These are all manifestations of the ego identifying with the Apollonian animus.

Conversely, at other times, the ego gets overwhelmed by the morbid shadow, feeling and seeing things that frighten her. The woman blurts out what she sees in an undifferentiated way or becomes mute, afraid to speak. She often induces Apollonian contempt or sadistic attack from others. And she fades to black.

In both cases, there is a lack of ego stability and containment. The woman is swept away either by animus or shadow. Analysis aims at building ego, which will be achieved largely through projective identification in the transference.

Transference takes hold quite readily, as noted earlier, due to the analysand's extreme extraversion, suggestibility and readiness to project power onto an authority figure. It is an idealized transference, the analyst quickly becoming the carrier of wisdom and enlightenment. The analyst's role is often that of counselor or teacher: helping test reality, discussing ways in which the analysand might improve her life, explaining the rules of the analytic frame. In this way, a therapeutic container is established and an ego alliance develops, which builds trust and promotes healing of the psychic split.

In this phase the analyst's function is much like that of Athena, who mediated between Apollo and the Furies at Orestes' trial. By upholding Apollonian values, the analyst wins the respect of the patient's animus, whose narcissistic contempt could shatter the idealized transference prematurely. Likewise, by a rational understanding of the patient's negative affects, the analyst allows room for the Furies and at least temporarily placates them, thereby neutralizing a possible massive negative transference reaction which could break the container. Thus the analyst stands for the words spoken by Athena to the Furies in *The Eumenides:*

> Thine heaviness myself will help thee bear.
> Older thou art than I, and surely ware
> Of wisdom than I wot not: yet also
> To me Zeus giveth both to think and know.[6]

---

[6] Aeschylus, *The Eumenides,* lines 847-850.

Athena with serpent.
(Seal stone, 5th cent. B.C.; Curium, Cyprus)

Demeter and Kore.
(Stone statue, Thebes; Louvre)

# 4

# Demeter/Persephone

*Wherever science dug shafts, cleared away layers of earth, penetrated caves, it always encountered this Goddess in the deepest strata.*
—Christa Wolf, *Cassandra.*

As the first level of trust develops, the nature of the transference begins to change. What started as a relationship with a good (albeit maternal) father, largely mental and based on rational understanding, evolves into a relationship with a good mother, more emotional and based on an empathic connection.

This change occurs subtly and organically. Over time the analyst proves to be trustworthy, withstanding attacks from the patient's animus and shadow without acting out induced reactions or retaliating. First-level resistances to transference and dependency are worked through. The analysand begins to see that she does not always have to mirror the object, that she has the capacity to generate her own reality and her own psychic material, and that others will relate to *her.*

One of Sarah's dreams illustrates this transitional phase:

Very vague—something about a flimsy, wispy material that is mine; it touches other people and wraps itself around them. It is sometimes pleasant to them, sometimes overwhelming, smothering, dangerous. Laurie and the lawyers [from the firm where she worked] are there. I realize, in amazement, that they serve the same kind of purpose which is to care for the material. Laurie helps pull out the material, and the lawyers pull it off when it gets dangerous.

Here is Cassandra—"she who entangles men."[1]

Sarah described the dream material as "thin and gauzelike, but it can get messy—sticky like cobwebs, gooey like mud or vomit. All these things, but it's just material." In the same session, she reported

---

[1] Graves, *Greek Myths,* vol. 2, p. 385.

that at work she was feeling more relaxed, better able to be herself and let out her "whiney, irritable, childish, crazy side." In the dream, the increasingly maternal analyst helps her let this infantile, polymorphous material come out and the lawyers, representing the Apollonian animus, pull it away when she is afraid she has gone too far.

This dream also reflects the analyst's changing role. There is less counseling and suggestion, more listening and mirroring; more feminine-mode receptivity, being instead of doing. The analyst allows the other to get under her skin. The analysand begins to use the analyst more. There may be requests for extra time or hysterical phone calls between sessions. I have found that in this phase I seem to have an abundance of patience and empathy. Synchronistically, it is usually possible to accommodate requests for more attention. Intrapsychically, the Cassandra woman's ego begins to disidentify from the animus and cathect, through projective identification, onto the analytic field, which is becoming more maternal.

As the analysand leaves the protection of the patriarchal defensive system and the maternal container constellates, fear, anxiety and even paranoid fantasies are aroused. As the libido regresses, there are often images of being devoured or swallowed up. While the woman experiences the joy of being seen and mirrored, she is terrified of becoming lost in *participation mystique*. It is therefore crucial in this phase that the analyst maintain a distinct observing ego and not allow herself to merge with the analysand or, worse, cause the latter to merge with and mirror her, as the analysand's mother did.

Jungian analyst Rosemary Gordon suggests that some of the patient's fantasied questions at this point are: Will the analyst hold safe the projected parts of me until I can integrate them myself? Or will she reject them? Or take them and not give them back to me?[2]

The role of the analyst here is much like that of a nursing mother whose mind and body are sensitive to the needs of her child but who, as an adult, must be sure she takes care of her own needs as well.

It becomes obvious that the underlying archetypal dominant here is Demeter/Persephone. This is what Micklem and Williams refer to.[3]

---

2 "The Concept of Projective Identification," p. 142.
3 See above, p. 72.

Demeter and Perspehone.
(Marble grave stele, early 5th cent. B.C., Pharsalus, Greece; Louvre)

But they see this mythologem as the problematic starting point. In fact, the Demeter/Persephone phase is a constructive developmental step, one that marks a therapeutic regression and the establishment, via the transference, of a positive maternal container which can eventually be introjected as feminine ego.

We remember Jung's observation that the hysteric's regression of libido culminates in a return to the womb—to the belly of the whale, in which Jonah saw the mysteries. This is illustrated in another dream of Sarah's:

> I have joined a club or society. I walk into the pool area where I now can go. It is a massive room with a huge pool, bigger than an Olympic pool, with very few swimmers. I am excited about it, but a little overwhelmed. Around a corner is a smaller pool—still very big—that is empty. It is a "kiddie pool," which I feel is more suitable for me.

This dream indicates a fully cathected transference: Sarah has joined the club. The swimming pool represents the analytic container holding the undifferentiated unconscious contents of the projection field. There are two pools. The huge one—the mother—is bigger than an Olympic pool. This indicates a regression beyond patriarchal collectivity back to the uroboric matriarchal state, perhaps to Gaia herself, the primal earth goddess. Sarah's joining the society foreshadows a psychological equivalent of initiation/rebirth such as took place in the Eleusinian Mysteries with their roots in the worship of the Great Mother.[4]

The dream also shows the dreamer's ambivalence, both her fear and excitement, over this prospect. At this stage both Ellen and Sarah expressed a fear that entering Jungian analysis is like joining a cult. Each one again revealed anxiety around deep dependency needs and the fear of losing personal identity through being swallowed up by the collective unconscious.

In the dream, the fact that there are only a few swimmers in the large pool emphasizes the club's exclusivity. It also indicates that

---

[4] See Marion Woodman, *The Owl Was a Baker's Daughter: Obesity, Anorexia Nervosa and the Repressed Feminine* (Toronto: Inner City Books, 1980), pp. 104-107.

some aspects of the dreamer are already in *participation mystique* with the mother/analyst. The dream ego, whether out of fear or an appropriate assessment of its size, prefers the kiddie pool. This suggests the dreamer's potential, through projective identification, to relate to the contents of the collective unconscious in a scaled-down, more personalized container.

Sarah took a concrete cue from this dream and started to swim on a regular basis. This was therapeutic on both a psychic and somatic level. Body work is crucial for the hysteric. Her animus-identified ego has created a mind-body split. Her new ego must be embodied in order to provide ballast and to enable her to process kinesthetic perceptions. Therefore she must get to know her body, strengthen it and become sensitive to its needs and cycles.

At this stage a woman may become preoccupied with body issues, such as hygiene, exercise and nutrition. She may take a new interest in clothes and her environment. Sarah, for example, who had always done everything she could to look plain, suddenly became concerned about her appearance. Signs of what was to become a beautiful woman began to show. She also reported a heightened sense of smell. As the analysand introjects the analyst's care for her well-being, she cathects to her own body and environmental field as if they were transitional objects.

In the transference arena, the analysand clings to the security of the analytic container. Any deviation in the frame at this time causes tremendous anxiety, threatening the rudimentary feminine ego with an overwhelming influx of negative affects.

The archetypal image underlying these transitional phenomena is the omphalos. This is the egg/womb/breast-shaped stone sacred to the Greeks and held to be the navel or center of the earth. There was one at Delphi, although the omphalos was originally sacred not to Apollo but to Gaia. Wherever Mother Earth was worshiped, there we may expect to find the omphalos.[5]

The suppliant was known to cling to the omphalos, reminiscent of the way an egg implants onto the uterus of a pregnant woman, obtaining sustenance from the highly vascular endometrium. In the

---

5 Harrison, *Themis*, pp. 396-399.

scene opposite, detail of a painting on a fourth-century B.C. terra cotta vase, we see Orestes in the sanctuary at Delphi, embracing the omphalos.

Psychologically, the omphalos can be viewed as an object representation of the good breast or womb, the positive mother, which seems to have the power to magically neutralize the negative mother, that is, keep the Furies at bay. One woman, borderline but with strong hysterical tendencies, had a pattern of grabbing and holding tight to her maroon leather purse when she became anxious and feared being overwhelmed by negative affects.

Likewise, although less concretely, the analytic container and the analyst also become the good objects to which the patient clings for protection against the morbid complex. In the early phases of analysis, the positive transference is able to absorb the attack by the shadow. But this does not last. The Furies are not really appeased, they are only temporarily placated.

It is worth repeating here that the phases of the analytic process are not linear but rather spiralic. Hysteria is characterized by remissions and exacerbations. Whenever the patient's ego is overwhelmed by an influx of unassimilable shadow material, the Demeter/Persephone phase is reconstituted in order to firm up the ego boundaries and stop the womb from wandering.

Naturally, the dark face of the goddess is not so easily dismissed. But after a positive maternal container is established, one is better prepared to meet this terrible aspect. Archetypally, Persephone becomes ready for the rape/initiation by Hades, so she can eventually take her place as queen of the underworld.

Orestes at Delphi.

Interior of the temple, showing the omphalos covered by a net of fillets. *Centre:* Orestes with the omphalos. *Upper left:* a dark Fury holds a serpent in outstretched hand. *Left of Orestes:* Apollo gestures with his right hand to expel the Fury. *Left:* Pythia fleeing the frightful sight. *Right:* Artemis overlooking the scene.

(Early Apulian volute krater, ca. 370 B.C.; Museo Nazionale, Naples)

Hecate, the threefold goddess.
(Museo Capitolino, Rome)

# 5

# Hecate

*Blessed is he who has seen things.*
—Hymn to Demeter.

What is the origin of the serpent in the Cassandra woman's paradise? Mythologically it was Zeus who allowed Hades, his brother and lord of the underworld, to take Persephone for his wife, but it is also known that Gaia conspired with Zeus. This hints at some grander plan, the blueprint of a larger opus, *coniunctio.*

In the Homeric *Hymn to Demeter,* Persephone tells her story:

> All of us were playing in a lush meadow, my friends and I . . . all virgins and full-bloomed in youth; we gathered the blossoms of earth in our hands, flower gathering flower—bouquets of gentle crocus, iris and hyacinth, rose buds and lilies, gorgeous to see. And there was a narcissus—the wide earth had brought it forth, glorious as a crocus, a jewel—and in ecstasy I spied it and plucked it, but the earth gave way beneath and from her burst the great lord Hades, who receives many. In his golden chariot, he carried me beneath the earth and I struggled all unwilling, screaming shrill a lament.[1]

Jane, in the process of losing her psychological maidenhood, had the following dream:

> I am walking through Central Park. A heavyset black man, off to the side, asks me for a match. I am afraid and try to ignore him. In a menacing voice he says, "Okay, then. This is where the sidewalk and the pavement end!"

This dream occurred in the fifth year of her analysis, which had been marked by a deep regression to the uroboric, paradisiacal level and the development of trust based on a symbiotic bond. The analysis had reconstituted in her a Pollyanna-like naiveté. The dream her-

---

[1] R. Wasson, C. Ruck and A. Hofmann, *The Road to Eleusis,* p. 71.

alded her loss of innocence, the need to separate from the mother and the concomitant irruption of an extreme negative transference.

Naturally, Jane was reluctant to leave the protective temenos of the maternal container, to face the darkness, especially her own negative affects and aggression.

In the dream, the woman refuses to provide a match for—that is, relate to or lend light to—her dark animus. Her ego prefers to stay on the pleasant, well-trodden path. At this point the animus turns nasty, threatening to forcibly take her away from her familiar world.

Psychologically, Hades functions to pull a woman out of the symbiotic merger with the mother and down into her dark depths, into experiences she would not willingly choose but which ultimately may lead to an expansion of consciousness. At the time, however, she only feels raped.

In this phase, Hades may be experienced by a woman through just such intruder dreams or through projection onto a man in her life or onto the analyst. Earlier in the process, the analysand learned to embrace a healthy narcissism—an embodied, holistic sense of herself, albeit inflated and grandiose—thereby healing what Melanie Klein calls the Cassandrian injured internalized object. In the glow of the unconditional Demeter container, the patient was able to feel entitlement and even greed, and often have her demands met.

But then, just as in Persephone's story where the narcissus gives rise to Hades "whom we all meet,"[2] there inevitably comes a time when the analyst feels the patient's demands as intrusive. Whether or not it is actually possible for her to meet these demands, the analyst feels that the woman wants too much.[3]

Archetypally, the analyst experiences an induction of Demeter's rage and grief for her paradise lost. The symbiosis has been broken.

---

[2] Ibid., p. 59.

[3] The negative countertransference here must be differentiated from one that is common to the first phase, in which the analyst's rejecting feelings are induced by the analysand's expectations that the analyst will be like her mother. This expectation can be interpreted as a resistance to the transference. However, the countertransference in the Hecate phase takes place on a deeper level. It grows out of the transference bond and can be viewed as the psychological contractions which mark gestational maturation and a readiness for rebirth.

When Sarah had to have emergency abdominal surgery, for example, she wanted me to be there with her. The hospital was quite far away and to me my presence seemed inappropriate. With mixed emotions I refused but continued to be in telephone contact. Nonetheless, my claiming my boundary aroused a tremendous amount of rage in Sarah. This marked a new phase in the transference. She was experiencing the terror and loneliness of Persephone raped by Hades, in this case the doctors penetrating her abdomen. Like Persephone, Sarah had cried out for help in an unconscious attempt to induce a Demeter-like response in me. When I did not rescue or protect her, she felt abandoned and betrayed.

This paradigm repeats itself in the countless boundary skirmishes of this third phase, which is marked by confusion and conflict. Analyst and analysand find themselves in adversarial positions for the first time. The basic pattern is as follows: The Cassandra woman makes a demand. The analyst holds firm to personal boundaries. The analysand feels that the analyst is withholding and experiences abandonment, rage and terror. The analyst confronts and describes these behavioral dynamics. The woman feels further misunderstood and enraged. Her narcissism has been penetrated. She feels attacked, raped, forced into the underworld of her own dark shadow. The analyst helps her work through her negative affects—rage, terror, grief and unrequited longing—and experience them consciously. Thus a healthy ego can displace the tendency to regress to her earlier Apollonian schizoid defenses.

The analyst neither complies with the woman's demands nor retaliates, though she understands and empathizes with the painful feelings. Although the Cassandra woman may feel deprived, she also feels seen. Because of that, she is willing to compromise. She can't have everything she wants, but she is willing to accept the limitations and take what she can get. Trust is maintained. The woman both hates and loves the analyst. The difficult separation-rapprochement phase of development is worked through and the depressive position negotiated. Thus separation becomes a rebirth in which something is lost and something is gained.

The analysand identifies with Demeter/Persephone, whose experience at Eleusis is "to be pursued, robbed, raped, to *fail to under-*

stand, to rage and grieve, but then to get everything back and be born again."[4] Because of her willingness to exert her power—to withhold her bounty and even be destructive—Demeter wins back her virginity. Like Demeter/Persephone, the woman must face the reality of her own dark shadow, wherein her deepest power lies.

Recall the cry that goes up at Eleusis, "Brimo bears Brimos!": Brimo, meaning the power to arouse terror, to rage, to roar or snort, yields Brimos, the horned child, representing both the new Persephone and Dionysus.[5] Thus the analysand experiences the negative affects of separation while internalizing her ego boundaries. An interior womb space is thereby created which can contain her ambivalence and from which she can give birth to an embodied chthonic animus that is able to assert his phallic power.

It is the analysand's new animus which does not hesitate to tell me when I have made an incorrect interpretation. This phallic power manifests not only in the analytic field but in the patient's outside life as well. At this stage, for instance, Sarah was able to confront her employers about being underpaid. She asked for and received a substantial raise. And Ellen finally left her unhappy marriage and made plans to move away from the depressed area of her home town to a bigger city.

Naturally, this phase has its own set of dangers and pitfalls. If the ego is not yet strong enough to assimilate the influx of negative affects released in the separation process, the woman may revert to her morbid schizo-hysterical defensive structure and/or break the analytic container.

At this stage, the analyst must be particularly careful not to act out a strong Hades induction. There might be a temptation to push an interpretation too far, penetrate too deeply or too fast, or maybe even give a sadistic twist to the knife. While Hades saw to it that Persephone ate of the pomegranate in order to ensure her return to the underworld, the modern woman may not be willing to tolerate such force-feeding. It constellates tremendous anxiety around the negative

---

[4] Jung and Kerényi, *Science of Mythology,* p. 137.
[5] Ibid., pp. 142-148.

mother complex for it smacks of her infantile eating experience when she was fed according to her mother's schedule.

It is no surprise that both Ellen and Sarah had severe feeding problems as infants. Sarah was passive and apathetic while Ellen suffered from colic and could only tolerate goat's milk. She remembers as a child hating to lean against her mother's breast. As an adult she has been plagued by a hypochondriacal fear of breast cancer.

As noted earlier, the mother of the Cassandra woman experiences her feminine identity through a merged state with her infant, but as dominatrix she demands that the child mirror *her* reality. She can tolerate no spontaneous emotional expression from the child. It only incites her own abandonment anxiety. If the baby is not compliant, the mother becomes confused, perhaps feels rejected and angry. If the baby cries, the mother might stuff the nipple back into her mouth, like Apollo spitting into Cassandra's. This is the "phallic" breast, feeding the baby with hidden aggression—too much, too fast and unrelated to the child's needs.

The child, meanwhile, withdraws into a schizoid state, burying all passions and strong affects. Certainly there is no room for her natural, devouring desirousness. She projects her field of consciousness into the psyche of the mother whom she can thereby safely mirror and contain, assuring herself as well as possible of a good and stable object. But the child thereafter remains in a disembodied, depersonalized state. She is a lost soul.

The bad/phallic breast is reconstellated at this stage, arising in the space created between analyst and analysand during the separation process. When the analyst does not meet all of her needs, the woman's negative affects are projected onto the transferential field; the analyst becomes the bad breast, recapitulating the patient's infantile experience of the negative mother. Insofar as she is unable to take responsibility for her own greed, rage and envy, the analysand feels overwhelmed and fears being devoured by the negative mother. It was at this stage in her process that Ellen remembered her childhood terror of toilets, the fear that when she flushed she would get sucked down into the dark swirling water.

The analyst must now help the analysand contain and process her painful experience. She becomes the "lavatory mother," accepting the

Cassandra woman's dark side, listening to her negativity—from her myriad of general complaints to pointed transferential hatred—without being destroyed or retaliating. This stage can be horribly painful for both parties, constellating loneliness, terror, rage, hatred and envy, plus the mutual projections, even paranoia, that result from the high degree of imaginal stimulation.

The archetypal dominant underlying the experience of the negative mother is Hecate, the patroness of Cassandra's own mother, Hecuba, who was reputed to be a witch.[6]

Hecate was originally a pre-Hellenic Great Mother, a goddess in her own right, ruling over the three realms of earth, heaven and sea. But she lost her identity with the virgin and mother aspects and consequently much of her power in patriarchal times.[7]

Angelyn Spignesi points out that "Hekate's early association with cosmic power and a high moral/spiritual function gave way in Greek religion to primarily chthonian associations."[8] Although Hecate retained her title as goddess of the moon and of childbirth, she took on evil connotations for the patriarchal Greeks. She became known as Daughter of the Night, goddess of the dark moon and black magic. She was the Giver of Visions, but also of madness and insanity. Worshiped at the crossroads, she was ritually placated to ward off all manner of evil. As Guide of Souls she was accompanied by ghosts as well as her daughters, the Furies and Cerberus, the three-headed dog who guards the underworld.

Hecate remained the patroness of magic and witchcraft even into the Christian era. By the Middle Ages, the witch was thought to be inimical to motherhood, notwithstanding the fact that in her contract with the devil (Hades), by which she "bodily and truly" conjoins with him, she becomes Persephone.[9]

The phallic breast itself is none other than the Witch's Tit. In *The Malleus Maleficarum* there is the following description of the way in which a witch obtains milk: The witch sits in a corner with a pail be-

---

[6] Graves, *Greek Myths,* vol. 2, pp. 341-343.
[7] Jung and Kerényi, *Science of Mythology,* p. 112.
[8] "Toward a Psychological Understanding of the Witch," p. 28.
[9] Ibid., p. 4.

tween her legs. She sticks a knife in the wall and gestures as though she were milking a cow. She sends her familiar to bring milk back from the udder of a neighbor's cow. The milk then emerges as if it were flowing from the knife. Thus a knife, one form of the witch's impersonal phallus, replaces the breast—"The witch's source of nurture came from a powerful weapon of action instead of a soft, receptive breast."[10]

It is not surprising that the Cassandra woman's experience of the Hecate aspect of her personal mother, herself a victim of the patriarchy, would be so negative. The following dream (Sarah's) is a striking illustration of the epiphany of the dark phallic goddess in the psyche of the modern Cassandra woman:

> I am upset and frenzied. I go to a room that is my room. I lie down on the floor. But the floor is made very badly of cheap, old wood. And I peer through the floorboards. Underneath is another floor— much more solid and well-made. There is an eruption from underneath and up through the old floor bursts a statue. It looks like a statue of the Virgin Mary but she is dressed in black. Her nose is long and wooden and also black. Her gown is ripped open, to reveal her breast, which is also black, and the left breast has been slashed open with a knife. The wound is fiery red and glowing, like a light that's coming from the inside. I am awed and frightened by this statue. I know it will disappear soon and I am afraid I will forget it. I want to tell Laurie about it and run to get a notebook to write down a description.

Sarah's upset and frenzied state is the hysteria with which her ego reacts when overwhelmed by the morbid complex. During this period she was experiencing a resurgence of hysterical symptomatology in response to an influx of separation anxiety.

In the second phase, Demeter/Persephone, Sarah had developed a stronger ego container; therefore in this dream she is able to go to her own room where she can become grounded and see what really supports her, namely the foundation whence springs the Black Madonna. Esther Harding tells us:

---

[10] Ibid., p. 14, citing Kramer and Sprenger, *The Malleus Maleficarum*, trans. Montague Summers (New York: Dover, 1971), p. 145.

There are in Europe to this day certain shrines of Mary, Mother of God, Moon of the Church, in which the image of Mary is black. These shrines of the Black Virgin are all wonder-working and are very highly esteemed, being visited by pilgrims from far and wide.[11]

With her great magical healing powers the Black Madonna is related to Hecate, goddess of the moon, especially in its dark waning aspect.

The dreamer knew nothing of the Black Madonna. Her unconscious was reaching into the collective stratum to repair the patriarchy's wounding of the dark feminine. It was to be a long time before Sarah would be able to relate to this epiphany. The archetypal form in which Hecate manifested in the dream—replete with phallic nose and breast and revealing the passions burning in her heart—shows how far these contents were from ego consciousness.

On the other hand, the goddess emerged auspiciously, an object of worship, appropriately eliciting a reaction in the dream-ego of awe, fear and an urgent interest in recording the event (a strong indication of eventual integration).

In order to benefit from the positive potential of the Hecate aspect, Sarah would have to work through the negative affects constellated by the separation process. It was crucial at that time that I use my own phallic power not as a weapon but as a source of fertility and growth, so that her afflicted relationship to Hecate, the crux of the Cassandra complex, could be healed.

Even though Hecate lost status under the patriarchy, she nonetheless was the only one of the Titans to be given a place among the Olympians. Zeus also allowed her to maintain her ancient power of granting every mortal's heart's desire. And sensitive she is to murmurs of the heart, able to hear what others cannot. It was in this capacity that Hecate could hear Persephone's screams as she was dragged down into the underworld. Here we can see Hecate as the patroness of analysts, priests, nurses and anyone else who bears witness to those moments in other people's lives when the veil between the upper and lower worlds lifts. Hecate, unlike Apollo, can relate to the darkest and wildest of emotions. She is familiar with

---

[11] *Woman's Mysteries,* p. 112. See also Marion Woodman, *The Pregnant Virgin: A Process of Psychological Transformation,* pp. 121-126.

depth and intensity. Alone in her cave, she has suffered and known abandonment.

Thus Hecate was the one to aid Demeter, comforting and mirroring her in her grief and helping her to win back her daughter. Demeter herself was by nature a gentle soul who rarely dealt harshly with others.[12] She was the good mother, whose love and care were unconditional and whose only fault, perhaps, was being overprotective. The loss of her daughter was more than she could bear. It was Hecate who stood beside Demeter, before Helios, demanding to know the truth about what had happened to Persephone. Thus Hecate helped Demeter to assert herself. According to the Homeric hymn, Demeter was later able to claim her own power by threatening

> to never again set foot on fragrant Olympus or let the earth bear fruit unless she saw her beautiful daughter with her own eyes. . . . by keeping the seeds hidden underground and so . . . cause the honors that are paid to the gods to perish.[13]

Hence Demeter withheld her bounty both from the gods and the race of men so that they too would feel the ravages of abandonment and would think twice before ever again presuming on her good nature. She set her limits, negotiated her boundaries, established the seasons.

Hecate played a crucial role in this development. As Phosphoros, the Torch-Bearer, she helped Demeter to see the dark truth by the reflective light of the moon and later became the constant servant and companion of the transformed Persephone, Queen of the Underworld. As goddess of childbirth, Hecate was the midwife in the Eleusinian Mysteries, helping Demeter to bear the birth pains of separation and also attending the rebirth of the virgin. As crone, Hecate added the third aspect, the dark element, to the mother-maiden dyad, thereby reestablishing the integrity of the primordial triune goddess.

Thus we see the positive potential of Hecate as she functions at Eleusis: bearing witness to Demeter/Persephone's darkest moments, comforting her in grief, helping her to see in the dark and to assert

---

[12] Graves, *Greek Myths,* vol. 1, p. 89.

[13] Wasson et al., *Road to Eleusis,* p. 68.

her will. It is this dark feminine experience which the analyst helps to mediate during the period in which the woman undergoes a psychological separation and rebirth. The analysand, like Persephone, experiences the depression and deflation inherent in losing her identification with the Demeter-analyst and not yet having introjected her own power.

It follows that envy arises in the transference, in the space that has been created by the separation process. The analyst still seems to have all the power and the analysand feels like the odd woman out, like Hecate disenfranchised, the third in a triangle.

At this point in the process, the triangle is pre-oedipal in nature, comprised of the ego and the split self-object representation—the good and bad breasts. The analysand experiences this self-object separation both intrapsychically and in projection onto the analyst. Anxiety arises around the dark side, which is as yet not fully integrated.

Both ontogenetically and phylogenetically, this dark aspect has been maligned and rejected. Now, in the analysis, it threatens the paradise of the good object connection. The woman experiences rage and envy around the fear that the hard-won analytic relationship may not be able to tolerate and incorporate the dark aspect. This dark aspect is the bisexual third thing, born out of the separation process. In other words, it is the Hecate-informed feminine ego and/or the Dionysus-informed animus.

There is undeniably pain associated with the loss of the symbiotic stage, but if the painful affects can be worked through and the depressive position negotiated, the gain is worth the loss. The trinity of the feminine Self can be reconstituted. The analysand must risk facing into and claiming her dark side in order to discover that the analytic container can hold, that there is room for her separate identity and that she can have power in her own right, as a woman and peer of the analyst.

The following two-part dream illustrates both the positive potential and the pitfalls inherent in the Hecate phase of therapy:

> I was in the bathroom and when I tried the door it was completely stuck and wouldn't open. I desperately fought, trying to open the door. I tried banging on the walls but my neighbors couldn't hear

me. I thought I was going to remain locked in my bathroom for the rest of my life. I was terrified. I realized that my panic wasn't helping so I sat down on the john lid. I realized that I was never going to open the door the way I had been pulling it; the only way was to trust my inner being and not be afraid. I was still skeptical, but I tried to relax and let my inner being encompass me, trusting whatever would happen—because for all I knew, I was still going to remain locked in the bathroom for the rest of my life. I went up to the bathroom door and got ready to tug at it. I put both my hands on the handle ready for a struggle and the door opened without effort. . .

A man was at a drawbridge gate banging on the door. A voice told him to try the bell. He rang the bell and the gate opened and he walked into a bustling medieval town. He went down a crowded street and stopped at a shoemaker's door. He entered a small room where there was a dark-haired, olive-skinned woman wearing a brown, hooded cape, sitting alone on a three-legged stool. The man went up to her. She told him that she mended souls. She was repairing a soul that had been split in half. It looked like she was sewing pieces of a heart together.

Part one of the dream reflects the schizo-hysterical pattern, characteristic of the initial phase of analysis, by which this patient, Anne, defends against the morbid complex. She retreats to a split-off place in her psyche where she can have her real emotions. She described the bathroom as "the most private and only warm room in the house." She would go there to cry. But the dream shows that what to her seems to be a safe container for negative affects becomes a prison in which she feels trapped.

Anne recalled that the night before she had closed the bathroom door to keep out Kitty, a friend's cat she had been taking care of. Thus she closes the door to the dark feminine shadow. Anne did not like cats. Her mother had told her that women are catty and therefore not to be trusted. "You never know when they are going to take a bite out of you or up and leave and say 'I've had enough!'" But when she closes the door to protect herself from the catty shadow, she ends up stuck in a prison of her own making. She cuts herself off from her deeper Hecateian nature which could help her deal with her painful emotions. Her ego has no other avenue but to become hysterical.

As the dream continues, however, she is able to sit down on the toilet seat and calm herself, trusting her inner being. The ability to contain her negative affects neutralizes the hysteria and allows her to escape from her schizoid prison. Thus she can open the door, no longer needing the bathroom complex to defend herself.

Part two of the dream shows, on an archetypal level, the constructive potential that such a personal accomplishment can yield. Bringing us full circle, this dream offers interesting counterpoints and even some resolutions to the images in one of Ellen's early dreams (page 79).

In Ellen's dream, the father rings the bell, calling the family to worship God the Father. In Anne's dream, a man rings a bell as well, but with a very different attitude and purpose. He is seeking entrance, not asking to be sought out as the central authority of the woman's psyche. The young man enters a bustling city, not the depressed, burned-out, decaying town of Ellen's dream.

In both cases, the animus leads us to Hecate imagery, which in Ellen's dream is in a state of fragmentation and in Anne's is not only whole and intact but is in human rather than cat form, thus closer to ego integration. The woman in the second part of Anne's dream, instead of being the source of overwhelming anxiety and hysteria, retains her darkness but functions creatively—mending souls, which echoes Hecate's titles as Guide of Souls and Fulfiller of Heart's Desires. As psychic cobbler, she binds the fragmented, catty shadow, grounding the ego by giving it a standpoint in the feminine Self. She is at once an image of the catty shadow and the dark aspect of the feminine, healing the split, making whole what has been broken.

In part one of Anne's dream, the dream-ego sits on the toilet, collects herself and connects to her inner being. In part two, the toilet becomes a three-legged stool, which also emphasizes the dark woman's mantic aspect, since the three-legged stool is a representation of the tripod. Therefore this feminine figure leads us right back to the Delphic Pythia and Cassandra herself.

Thus we see that Hecate is the core of the Cassandra woman's problem and the archetypal image behind mediality.

The name for the ancient goddess religion of Northern Europe was Wicca or Wekken, meaning to prophecy; witches were known to have second sight.[14] The word *wych* in Anglo-Saxon means pliant.[15] It is this medial aspect of the witch that the authors of the *Malleus* describe when they list the qualities of the woman who yields to the devil: They are "more impressionable, and more ready to receive the influence of a disembodied spirit." They are fluid, not private and contained. They have "slippery tongues and are unable to conceal from their fellow-women those things which by evil art they know." The witch is a serpent who goes underground, sucks in the devil in her darkness and then merges with other human beings. She is "more bitter than death" because she acts as the medium through which the devil can get to earth to contaminate men. A woman's emotions—her "inordinate affections and passions"—are likened to the "heaving and boiling" tides of the sea, which is the reason why all kingdoms of the world have been overthrown by women.[16]

The medieval inquisitors believed that witches were given to unnatural acts. Nothing could have been further from the truth. The English word witch and the German equivalent *Hexe* mean wise woman and her wisdom or knowledge is specifically *about* nature.

According to Spignesi, "witches were consciously training their souls to enter into the intimate relation between the waning and waxing, creating and destroying rhythms of nature." Their craft involved a thorough understanding of nature, of "the ebb and flow of the numinous instinctual forces in tide, harvest, herd."[17] And they used this knowledge for healing and to insure fertility.

The witch was very much mother, but in a transpersonal sense, "not through personally bearing and caring for babies, yet in her mothering of the earth."[18] The witch worships Mother Nature in both her life-giving and death-dealing aspects. And she is involved on all the levels in which nature manifests—physical, emotional and spiritual. If she has a cold-blooded, snakelike quality, it is because of her interest in these transpersonal collective forces. Through the

---

[14] Spignesi, "Witch," pp. 16-17.

[15] Ruth Ross, *Irish Trees* (Dublin: Eason & Son, 1980), p. 10.

[16] Spignesi, "Witch," pp. 5-7, citing Kramer and Sprenger, *Malleus Maleficarum*, pp. 43-44.

[17] Ibid., pp. 16-17.

[18] Ibid., p. 31.

practice of magic she learns to harness this natural power and consciously direct it, in order to achieve her will and penetrate beyond the veil of exoteric reality to see into the dark shadows that lie beyond.

At this point in the Cassandra woman's process, the witch can constellate positively within the analytic container. The Cassandra woman is no longer, as in the Demeter phase, identified with the projection field which has now itself become a third thing between analyst and analysand. It is very exciting and rewarding when, after the rage and envy of separation have been weathered, analysand and analyst, in a strange new therapeutic alliance, become two witches, as it were, stirring their caldron. It is within this caldron that all the images and affects go through their permutations and transformations. The two stir and cackle and wait and watch. They see together and learn and teach each other the "magickal" art.

It is in this phase that the Cassandra woman really tastes her own creative potential and learns that she need not only meet others' expectations, like Demeter providing the world with her bounty. She gets to know her own value and power and how to use it to get what she wants. But in order to create her own future, she must be able to see the present even in its darkest reality, believe what she sees and have the courage of her convictions. She must consciously envision the way she wants things to be and harness the energy to achieve her goals. That is the essence of magic.

But this phase can also be dangerous. I remember a moment in Sarah's very first session when her normally blue eyes took on a distinctly greenish glow. I thought, "This woman is a witch!" The phenomenon did not occur again until years later, during the Hecate phase. And it was important to the process that I could witness her envy and rage, her capacity for evil and destructiveness, her lust for power and desire to be queen. My seeing her in this way had several consequences: her dark side was mirrored, thus helping her to claim her power; I became a role model for her believing what she sees; and I was able to protect myself from her as yet unbridled negative energies.

In this phase, a woman can fall into a state of identification with Hecate as the dark aspect of the feminine Self. Jane's dream illustrates this inflation:

I am staying at a house in the country. I go to look for my husband. I can't find him. I look out the kitchen window. I see that it will soon be dawn. There is a deck outside the kitchen. I see my husband there lying on a mattress with his [adult] daughter [from a previous marriage). I am furious. I get some scissors. I open them up and get ready to stab him in the heart.

The environment of this dream, a house in the country, represents an ego that has found a place in the natural setting of the instinctual mother-world. Jane described the area as "rural, woody—not suburban, but not the deep boondocks." It is a borderline place. The house does not belong to her; she is renting it, implying that she has accessed this material within the analytic container and has yet to make it her own.

Clearly, in the three years since her dream of the heavyset black man (page 95), Jane has encountered her dark side. The daughter in this dream represents the dreamer's incestuous relationship to the patriarchal animus from the old psychological order, still present in the shadows.

One of the painful truths that the Cassandra woman sees at this stage is how she has been betrayed by the patriarchy. Long ago, she had given up her essential feminine identity and power to assure herself of a place in the father's heart, but in fact he had little interest in her other than in how she could help him feel good about himself. Recall the observation by Christa Wolf's Cassandra: "He knew his ideal of me; that was supposed to hold still."[19]

Now the analysand is ready to face the dissolution of the oedipal delusion that she is Daddy's girl, the final shattering of the father-daughter collusion and the useless narcissism of her Apollonian animus. She no longer wants a man or an animus who patronizes her, demands obeisance and disallows any challenge to his authority. She wants a consort who will relate to *her,* even in her darkest hues. In the process of analysis, she has made a solid ego-based connection to

---

[19] See above, p. 32.

the feminine Self and the chthonic Dionysian animus who can help her overthrow the stifling patriarchal order. Likewise, since she has experienced the deflation of separation and can stand on her own two feet, she can afford to feel her rage.

Even though the woman may have the courage of her convictions, there may still be a strong resurgence of separation anxiety—an influx of guilt, fear and inferiority—when she breaks the collusive merger with the father. She experiences the self-loathing which is a result of the internalization of the patriarchy's view of the woman who owns her dark power. This is the view expounded by Apollo in *The Eumenides* when he describes the Furies as follows:

> The Virgins without love,
> So grey, so old, who never god above
> Hath kissed, nor man, nor from the wilderness
> One wild beast. They were born for wickedness
> And sorrow; for in evil night they dwell,
> And feed on the great darkness that is Hell,
> Most hated by the Gods and human thought.[20]

When the woman gives up being the father's daughter, she faces her aloneness, feels unloved and unlovable, like Hecate's daughters, the Furies, who have been abandoned, rejected and maligned for thousands of years. But most of all she feels the Furies' rage at the patriarchy, invoking the power of the dark goddess: "Hear thou my wrath, O Mother, Night, mine own!"[21]

This is the power, as revealed in Jane's dream, that energizes the third, the other woman, in the love triangle. For no sooner are the perils of the pre-oedipal triangle negotiated than the oedipal triangle itself raises its ugly head. Then the woman will not hesitate to use her power for revenge or justice, and to achieve her goal. Thus we have an identification with the negative mother herself, Clytemnestra, who not only acts out her envy of Cassandra but also avenges Agamemnon's sacrifice of her daughter Iphigenia and ultimately reestablishes

---

20 Aeschylus, *The Eumenides,* lines 68-74.
21 Ibid., line 843.

matriarchal supremacy through a reenactment of the ancient fertility ritual, slaughter of the year-king.[22]

The oedipal triangle can manifest clinically in many ways. The analysand may go through a serious man-hating phase, especially taking offense at men who represent the patriarchal establishment. In the transference, there may be a distrustful, envious preoccupation with the analyst's outside life, spouse or other analysands. Or she may get furious if the analyst makes an interpretation which seems to come out of an Apollonian view, distant and emotionally unrelated.

In Jane's dream, the woman takes murderous revenge on the husband/animus for preferring the daughter's company. Her weapon is a mundane sewing tool, but it is also the attribute of the third of the Fates, who has the power to cut the cord, the thread of life, of the patriarchal merger. She opens the scissors like she opens her legs, to see the truth with her third eye, the dark vaginal eye of the goddess. Thus she aims to kill the patriarchy. Her identification with matriarchal power is consolidated. The goddess reigns supreme.

This is a frightening and bloodthirsty image, but one which, ironically, carries with it the promise of an eventual dawning of solar consciousness for the woman. By her refusal to feed the collusive father-daughter tie once and for all, there arises the potential for the transformation of narcissistic Apollo and eventually a genuine union of opposites.

Hecate.
(Engraved gem, Rome)

---

[22] Graves, *Greek Myths,* vol. 2, p. 56.

Artemis.
(From Walter F. Otto, *The Homeric Gods*, p. 73)

# 6

# Artemis

The violent imagery of the Hecate phase can be terrifying to us with our patriarchal sensibilities and taboos. At times it is difficult to believe there is any redeeming value in the pain and horror of a psychic situation that is often a worse hell than what originally brought one into therapy.

What are we really afraid of? That we might never return from the underworld? That we cannot survive our deepest passions and instincts? Does the moon involute when it reaches its apogee of darkness, swallowing itself up like a black hole? Yes, disasters occur. But ordinarily nature takes its course. The moon waxes again. In our modern world, in which Mother Nature is not respected and we no longer live close to her rhythms, we may not trust in her ebb and flow. We may be afraid of drowning in our own emotional tides.

In fear of the destructive power of the waning moon, the patriarchy banished the dark goddess to her underground cave. But this repression only served to cut off the Hecate aspect from the light of ego consciousness and manufactured, in the manner of a self-fulfilling prophecy, a vortex of negativity. Thus Hecate becomes evil and can no longer exercise her positive creative capabilities.

At ancient Eleusis, torch in hand, Hecate lit Persephone's way back to the upperworld to rejoin Demeter, thereby reconstituting the goddess' triune wholeness. But as a result of patriarchal fragmentation, the goddess lost her integrity. Artemis Magna Mater shed her orgiastic aspect to become the uptight tomboy of Hellenic Greece. She was the little girl sitting on her daddy Zeus's knee; when asked by him what presents she would like, she wished for "eternal virginity; as many names as my brother Apollo; a bow and arrows like his."[1]

Hecate might even hate this Olympian Artemis, aspiring to be a man and giving up her primordial virginity for the pristine patriarchal version. In a culture which devalues dark feminine power and wisdom, the crone envies the maiden instead of helping her; the waning moon hates the waxing moon; the left hand of the goddess fights against the right. Nature cannot be trusted.

We can see how this patriarchal fragmentation of the goddess creates strife within the collective feminine psyche. Divide and conquer. The young pure virgin and the long-suffering, self-sacrificing *mater dolorosa* are put on a pedestal; the sexually active woman and the witch are despised. The Old Testament asks, "Who can find a virtuous woman?" Even the root of the word virtuous connotes that a woman has value only insofar as she is related to the man *(vir)*. The woman who generates her own power, as seductress or crone, is wicked.

With the legacy of such a split, the modern woman who finds herself called to mediate Hecate has a hell of a time of it. She may experience maidenhood and motherhood (if she ever becomes a mother) as confusing and unfulfilling. Her mediality is more a liability than an asset. She uses her shape-shifting ability merely to conform to others' expectations. Because she does not have a strong feminine ego with which to deal with the Hecate aspect, her charisma is a source of chaos rather than creative power, and her dark visionary eye foments the unconscious instead of raising consciousness. But if she can work through the patriarchal introjects of self-loathing and prejudice against the crone, she has a good chance of gaining a positive relationship to the Hecate aspect in the second half or, more appropriately for a woman, the third third, of life. This suggests a good prognosis for the woman who seeks analysis after fifty.

We know that Hecate constellates at the crossroads, which is where her shrines were traditionally found. This reflects the potential for a woman to experience the dark feminine whenever she finds herself at a psychological nexus, when she has choices to make. The

---

[1] Graves, *Greek Myths,* vol. 1, p. 83.

Cassandra woman in the Artemis phase is at such a crossroads. Previously, she plunged into her dark depths, but in order to make use of the power she has found there she must be able to incorporate her experience into ego-consciousness. This is a crucial time. Any path she might take has its own set of perils, but some truly lead to disaster. She has basically three choices.

She can choose the left-hand path of black magic, which is the abuse of power for personal gain and the result of inflation and identification with the dark side of the Self. A woman stuck here may find herself tortured with nightmares or phobias of being burned, strangled or drowned, the three most common forms of execution of witches in the Middle Ages.[2] This state of identification with Hecate kicks up memories from the collective unconscious, perhaps an inner attempt to compensate for the psychic inflation. If the Cassandra woman cannot process these compensatory phenomena and take responsibility for abusing her power, she may be swallowed up in the negative vortex, destroying herself and others.

In the face of these nightmarish terrors, the woman may opt for the second alternative, to go back on the road whence she came.[3] It may seem too scary and overwhelming for her to own the power. But a regression like this would only perpetuate the neurotic state, reconstitute the morbid complex and increase the danger of her drowning in the emotional tides that have already been set in motion.

The only viable conscious choice is to take the right-hand path in the direction of continuing to claim her feminine power but learning to work with it in a disciplined fashion, responsibly and morally. This is the path of white magic, the use of power for the greater good and not just for personal gain. It is far from inflationary and in fact requires the conscious differentiation of ego and Self.

I discussed magic earlier, in describing the Hecate phase. Here we must take a closer look at this term. The concept of magic is one which is widely misunderstood. We all practice magic every day of our lives, whenever we carry an idea to fruition. And yet the word

---

[2] The execution of witches by strangulation may relate to the phenomenon of the *globus hystericus*.

[3] Jung calls this a regressive restoration of the persona. See *Two Essays in Analytical Psychology*, CW 7, pars. 254ff.

itself still carries a stigma as well as supernatural connotations. Because it cannot be rationally explained in terms of cause and effect, magic remains a mystery, and therefore a threat to our Apollonian minds, imbued with a need to understand and thus master our world. This xenophobic prejudice produces a collective fear and distrust which precludes the ability to differentiate between black and white magic. Then we either reduce magic to infantile wish-fulfillment or attack it as evil.

In *The Spiral Dance,* magic is defined as "the art of sensing and shaping the subtle, unseen forces that flow through the world, of awakening deeper levels of consciousness beyond the rational."[4] Its practice is conscious and ego-based, involving study and hard work:

> To work magic is to weave the unseen forces into form. . . . The power of magic should not be underestimated. It works, often in ways that are unexpected and difficult to control. But neither should the power of magic be overestimated. It does not work simply, or effortlessly; it does not confer omnipotence. "The art of changing consciousness at will" is a demanding one, requiring a long and disciplined apprenticeship.[5]

The Cassandra woman may be instinctively drawn to the esoteric disciplines which offer the benefit of an already established body of knowledge, steeped in ancient tradition and a strong moral code. Whether via Wicca, Kabbalah, yoga or analytic psychology, she can learn techniques of ritual and meditation, how to harness elemental energies and direct her will to bring down the image from the astral place into material manifestation.[6] According to Starhawk,

> "Will" is very much akin to what Victorian schoolmasters called "character": honesty, self-discipline, commitment, and conviction.

---

[4] Starhawk, *The Spiral Dance: A Rebirth of the Ancient Religion of the Great Goddess,* p. 13. This definition of magic must be clearly differentiated from the psychological term, which refers to the pre-separatio, magical level of the psyche. The practice of magic springs from and is guided by the same principles, such as identification and *pars pro toto*. But the two are not the same, any more than merger is identical to empathy.

[5] Ibid., p. 109.

[6] She may also learn these lessons through the discipline of some creative art form.

Those who would practice magic must be scrupulously honest in their personal lives. In one sense, magic works on the principle that "It is so because I say it is so . . ." For my word to take on such force, I must be deeply and completely convinced that it is identified with truth as I know it. If I habitually lie to my lover, steal from my boss, pilfer from supermarkets, or simply renege on my promises, I cannot have that conviction.

Unless I have enough personal power to keep commitments in my daily life, I will be unable to wield magical power. To work magic, I need a basic belief in my ability to do things and cause things to happen. That belief is generated and sustained by my daily actions. . . . Of course, life is full of mistakes and miscalculations. But to a person who practices honesty and keeps commitments, "As I will, so mote it be" is not just a pretty phrase; it is a statement of fact.[7]

Thus magic can be seen as a developed form of the power of positive thinking. The occult tradition can provide a container for the Cassandra woman's magical practice, teaching discrimination, the difference between Self and ego, and that one must suffer the consequences of one's actions. "What you send, returns three times over."[8]

While Hecate was the patroness of magic and witchcraft in the Middle Ages, in ancient Greece it was her moon-sister and alter-identity, Artemis, who was known for training covens of women with strict discipline. The modern Cassandra does well to learn Artemis's lessons, for this goddess can provide some very important tools for the medial woman.

Artemis is the archetypal role model for this phase because the complexity of her multilevel nature offers great potential for psychological differentiation. Not only was Artemis a fierce guardian of women's mysteries but she was also able to adapt to the changing of the gods. In matriarchal times, she was worshiped as the Great Mother, akin to the Cretan Lady of the Wild Things. The Olympian Artemis retained her identity as the triple moon goddess, incorporating Selena and Hecate. She continued to be worshiped in her nymph

---

7 Starhawk, *Spiral Dance*, p. 111.

8 Ibid., p. 12.

aspect, as "an orgiastic Aphrodite with a male consort," only in more remote regions such as Ephesus.[9] Thus Artemis provides a whole image of the feminine Self, both the dark occult aspect and her more popular face, as Maiden of the Silver Bow, Apollo's loving twin.

One could say that Artemis adapted to patriarchal times by identifying with the aggressor. She learned to fight and hunt even better than a man. She perfected her skill with bow and arrow, which she used both offensively, to hunt her prey, and defensively, to ferociously guard her territory.

But with Artemis, appearances can be deceiving. On the face of it, she was man's faithful comrade at arms. inspiring the most woman-fearing male with trust because of her independence and integrity, standing her ground at any cost and defending her virginity to the death. But meanwhile, hidden in her secret grove, she continued to perform her ancient matriarchal rites. This was the goddess who demanded blood, even human sacrifice, and would not hesitate to punish those who neglected her. It was Artemis whom the Hellenes continued to propitiate at weddings because of her ancient hostility toward patriarchal monogamous marriage. And it was she who turned the hapless Actaeon, when he espied her in her nakedness, into a stag subsequently torn to pieces by his own dogs.[10]

Of all her manifold attributes, it may be Artemis's ability to protect herself that is most valuable for the Cassandra woman to learn. For the goddess was able to translate her virginity into not only self-containment but also the capacity to veil herself. Artemis may well be the most occult of all the goddesses of the Greek pantheon. What appeared to be her extreme impenetrability and immovability may in fact have been a most ironic form of magical shape-shifting, like a witch's glamor, creating an illusion of coldness and distance. In the privacy of her sacral space, her feminine passions ran deep. Perhaps she knew how dangerous it was to be seen and how important to hide her power and not flaunt it in the face of a still insecure patriarchy.

---

[9] Graves, *Greek Myths,* vol. 1, p. 85.

[10] Ibid., pp. 84-85, 225, 268.

Learning the lessons of Artemis gives the Cassandra woman a persona with which to veil and thus protect herself from patriarchal attack. She also acquires strong ego boundaries which enable her to differentiate between what is her own personal experience and what is collective. She is then able to close off her medial apparatus except when she chooses to keep it open. This ego integrity not only helps her avoid being victimized by the constant influx of unconscious material, from without and within, but also creates the feminine container in which the longed-for *coniunctio* can eventually take place. One must be able to say no before one can safely say yes. And who knows how to say no better than Artemis, the great nay-sayer, herself?

A dream of Sarah's illustrates the need for the Cassandra woman to consciously integrate the lessons of Artemis:

> I am living at the university, studying piano in preparation for a recital. It is possible for me to give a great performance, but only if I give my full attention to practicing. I hear the potential recital in my head. It's the Haydn sonata that I love. Cassie is living there too. There is the feeling of constant interruption, so much to do. I have to go to swimming class and I have to do things with Cassie.

In the dream, Sarah finds herself back at the university which was where "the cool kids used to hang out in high school." But Sarah always felt uncomfortable, like an outsider. She never felt part of her peer group. Perhaps now with the help of Artemis, patroness of the feminine latency group, Sarah has another chance to work through this developmental phase during which the feminine ego-identity consolidates. Likewise, she can learn the skills necessary to succeed in the patriarchal world.

The recital represents the task at hand, which requires fluency in both masculine and feminine modes. Thus we see an early *coniunctio* image. The Haydn sonata represents perfect Apollonian form which, according to Sarah, one must play with "control but also let the feeling come out."

The piano represents the medial "instrument" Sarah is learning to play. She had seen on television a child prodigy who said, "I can say things with my violin that I can't say any other way." Sarah imagined that she was the mother of such a child, nurturing her gift and still protecting her childhood. This is the attitude that she has needed to have toward her own inner child.

It was at this time that Sarah resumed the acting classes she had dropped five years earlier, before she began analysis. She associated the dream image of playing the piano with acting, which involves, she said, "making people feel the magic in the performance space: all you need to do is create a frame for the audience. It's like a shaman thing."

In the dream, Sarah hears the potential recital in her head. This is the first step in the magical process—getting the image clear. But to bring that potential into physical reality involves hard work and discipline. Otherwise the venture remains a narcissistic fantasy. It had been her inability to deal with the vicissitudes of her studies, especially the humiliation of facing up to her own mistakes and inferiorities, that had caused Sarah to quit acting. She did not have a strong enough ego to endure the mortification. Now, when she returned to acting class, Sarah was able to use it as an arena in which she could practice her skills and develop discipline, while also learning to relate to her peer group.

The dream indicates what is necessary if Sarah is to accomplish her goal. She must practice and work hard, focusing on the task at hand. She must organize her life, set priorities. She must also go to swimming class, which is to say her embodied ego must become more proficient in the water, the medial element. This idea is consistent with the fact that part of Sarah's educational experience involves doing things with Cassie, who is in fact a real-life friend of hers. Not only is her name derivative, but her personality is also quite Cassandra-like. Thus Sarah must continue to work with her Cassandra shadow. For example, she must learn to say no to extraneous social obligations, to hold her own and not just get sucked into being and doing what others want from her. (In a later dream, we will see more specifically what Sarah needs to do with Cassie.)

Of course Artemis also gets constellated in the analytic relationship, which at this point is actually much like that of the Athena phase at the beginning of the process, in that there is less projective identification and more distance between analyst and analysand.

Again there is a teaching/learning mode—communication rather than communion—but now it is like a seminar rather than a lecture.

In this phase the analyst takes her role from Artemis. The content of the sessions is concerned not so much with the general activities of daily life but is rather more specific, personal and physical, often relating to aspects of feminine reality—somewhat like a woman's consciousness-raising or assertiveness training group from the 1970s. Much time is spent discussing the vicissitudes of work and discipline, and learning the art of fighting and self-defense (both physical and psychological). Body work, especially if it involves a competitive sport, is an excellent way to practice these skills.

At this time the analysand may go through a period of being touchy and belligerent, even with the analyst. She is superconscious of when her boundaries are being violated. For example, one day Ellen stormed into her session and greeted me with, "Go fuck yourself!" Referring to her last session in which I had cautioned her against using drugs, she told me not to tell her what to do and that I sounded like her mother judging her. "It feels like a put-down; and I want to make my own mistakes." Analysis was only one of many places in her life where she was ferociously claiming her own boundaries, clearly an important step for a woman whose mediality had nearly destroyed her.

On the other hand, Ellen's behavior revealed a lack of discipline and containment. Some months later, she had a dream which indicated a development in this area:

> I am at summer camp. I am walking over a hill and I see three vicious black dogs who are trying to get at me. But a man is holding them back from biting me.

This dream takes place at camp, the setting where Artemis trains her covens. Like Sarah, Ellen had a negative latency peer group experience. She hated camp: "It was like a prison to me. I felt totally lost. I was so wishy-washy, I had no identity." Again like Sarah, Ellen has an opportunity to repair this experience.

Now the problem, as revealed in the dream, is the vicious dogs, representing Hecate and/or the wild aspect of Artemis. The dogs are there to guard the camp, that is to defend the feminine ego boundaries from being violated. But these forces can also turn destructively on the ego. The animus, described by Ellen as "a good-looking blond guy who is part of the camp," functions to restrain this wild aspect.

The archetypal dominant underlying the animus in this phase is of course Apollo himself, Artemis's twin brother. But here Apollo is still in his intermediate Homeric form—the heroic snake-slayer—and, as such, is identified with Heracles, Defender from Evil.[11] In fact, the dream image is specifically reminiscent of Heracles' twelfth labor when, after being initiated into the Lesser Mysteries at Eleusis, Heracles descended to the underworld. Robert Graves describes the scene:

> Persephone . . . came out from her palace and greeted Heracles like a brother. . . .
>
> When Heracles demanded Cerberus, Hades, standing by his wife's side, replied grimly: "He is yours, if you can master him without using your club or your arrows." Heracles found the dog chained to the gates of Acheron, and resolutely gripped him by the throat—from which rose three heads, each maned with serpents. The barbed tail flew up to strike, but Heracles, protected by the lion pelt, did not relax his grip until Cerberus choked and yielded. . . .
>
> Heracles dragged Cerberus, bound with adamatine chains, up a subterrene path. . . . As Cerberus resisted, averting his eyes from the sunlight, and barking furiously with all three mouths, his slaver flew across the green fields and gave birth to the poisonous plant aconite, also called hecateis [Wolf Bane], because Hecate was the first to use it.[12]

Thus the power which once belonged to the realm of the Dionysus animus is now under the control of the Heracles animus and closer to ego-consciousness. Many of Heracles' feats were aimed at taming the wild beast. He proves to be a healthy heroic animus because he is so related to the feminine. Upon his death Heracles was adopted by Hera who, according to Graves, "loved him next only to Zeus":

> Heracles became the porter of heaven, and never tires of standing at the Olympian gates, towards nightfall, waiting for Artemis's return from the chase. He greets her merrily, and hauls the heaps of prey

---

[11] Harrison, *Themis*, p. 378.
[12] Graves, *Greek Myths*, vol. 2, p. 154.

out of her chariot, frowning and wagging a finger in disapproval if he finds only harmless goats and hares. "Shoot wild boars," he says,"that trample down crops and gash orchard-trees; shoot man-killing bulls, and lions and wolves! But what harm have goats and hares done us?"[13]

Thus Heracles, in loving comradeship, exhorts Artemis to discriminate and set limits on her aggressive, destructive nature.

We see in one of Ellen's dreams a further aspect of the limit-setting function of the animus as well as an image of the ego-Self axis which constellates in the Artemis phase:

I need a place to live in New York City. Cassandra lets me stay at her apartment. I want to clean up her dirty kitchen to show my appreciation. I want to get the feeling of living in a New York City apartment with a roommate. Her husband comes, although they don't live together yet. I ask him about washing the kitchen towels. He says to be careful because there is only so much water and the washer's been running all day.

The Cassandra in this dream is very different from the one that appeared in Sarah's dream during the Athena phase (page 81). Sarah's Cassandra Castleglove represented the state of the complex at the beginning of the process, split off from ego consciousness and functioning largely as a defensive structure. Ellen's Cassandra symbolizes the complex as it has evolved, still representing unassimilated shadow but now having more of the properties of the feminine Self.

Cassandra was in fact the name of a woman Ellen knew personally. They had gone to the same high school but only became friends after Cassandra divorced her husband and moved back to their home town to open her own business. Ellen described this woman as an interesting and genuine person, "a success story, I really like her." She had had a difficult life, but was not destroyed by it. She had the courage to leave an unhappy marriage in which her husband, like Apollo, ran around with other women. She had the vision and fortitude to build a new life for herself. And eventually she met a man who loved and supported her.

---

13 Ibid., p. 203.

In many ways this story parallels the development of the Cassandra woman. At first, she is in thrall to the macho animus which does not really care about her. Breaking free of the destructive tie, she returns home to her feminine ground, working hard to establish herself as an individual (as virgin, in a psychological sense). Finally, she finds a true partner.

The dream shows us that the Cassandra shadow is apparently alive and well and living in New York. The move is still somewhat beyond the dream-ego's reach, but the will is there. The dream suggests that the ego needs to live closer to and be more grounded in the Self, which is still in projection and in large part carried by the analyst. In fact it is the analyst, not Ellen's friend Cassandra, who lives in New York, which adds a transferential dimension to the dream. By withdrawing the projection and integrating the Cassandra shadow, Ellen can get access to New York, the collective hub which represents the Self, the real value of her analysis, and expanded life opportunities.

The action in this dream takes place prior to *coniunctio*. Cassandra and her husband do not yet live together. There is an implication that Ellen needs to move in first. In other words, the ego needs to be more related to the shadow before the union can be consummated. The ego needs to do some work, to clean up the dirty kitchen.

A kitchen is where food is cooked. Psychologically, it is where unconscious contents are alchemically transformed. Cleaning the kitchen is a necessary maintenance task which creates order out of chaos. It is not the kind of work that is immediately appealing; most of us find it routine and mundane, perhaps even demeaning. Thus it requires humility, responsibility and discipline. The ego acts as the sorceress's apprentice.

The dream indicates Ellen's willingness to grapple with the dirt, which represents the less attractive aspects of the Cassandra shadow, namely the sense of inferiority and envy, and the fear that she cannot meet the demands of the Self. By dealing with these affects, she can relate directly to the Cassandra living within her instead of idealizing and projecting her. This mortifies the Cassandra aspect in further preparation for *coniunctio*.

Ellen described her friend Cassandra as a woman who was somewhat inflated, relating to her fiancé, several years younger than herself, as to a son-lover. The ego's clean-up provides an opportunity to reduce the inflation, enabling a future relationship to the animus on a more equal basis.

In her dream, the animus warns Ellen not to use too much water. He advocates moderation and sets limits. Since water is the medial element, he draws a boundary around her tendency to be boundaryless. By implication, the animus is exhorting her not to use limitless *solutio* to clean away the dirt, pointing out a regressive tendency to drown painful affects in a merged state of *participation mystique.* She needs to scrub, grapple with the dirt, deal consciously with her affects. Less water and more elbow grease, more assertive ego work, are in order.

This dream heralded Ellen's move to the big city several years later. Psychologically, she was able to internalize her projected image of the feminine Self, seeing herself as the author of her own destiny. Still, she retained an awareness of the attendant responsibilities and anxieties: working, living without a man and raising her children on her own.

During this process Ellen acquired a positive animus that can help her to discipline and assert herself. The analyst, as comrade and coach, also mediates the role of the positive animus, discussing goals, tactics and the rules of the game. This is Apollo who is brother and comrade of Artemis. Thus the Apollonian animus reemerges in the psyche of the Cassandra woman as familiar and related.

After all, Artemis and Apollo were contained in the same womb. And they had much in common—both *Lykeios,* avid hunters, able to shoot straight with bow and arrow. It is in their more primitive aspects that they find their common ground and it is upon this common ground that they accomplished numerous mythological tasks. Together, they slew the children of Niobe, built the horned altar at Delos and fought against the Greeks in the Trojan War.[14] This brother-sister relationship manifests intrapsychically, at this phase in the process, as ego and animus working together as a team.

---

[14] Graves, *Greek Myths,* vol. 1, pp. 258-259.

We see further evidence of this team effort in the illustration on page 93, which depicts Orestes at Delphi. Artemis's presence implies that she joined with Apollo in supporting another brother-sister pair, Orestes and Electra, in their effort to put an end to the matriarchy but also to exonerate the matricide. This is corroborated in variations of the myth in which Orestes is purified in Artemis's temple. In another version, the only way Orestes could be freed from the Furies was by bringing to Greece the statue of Taurean Artemis, which was said to have fallen from heaven in prehistoric times.[15] Psychologically, this reflects the animus function of taming the wild beast and suggests that Orestes could neutralize the Furies by gaining control of Artemis's wild, primordial, orgiastic aspect.

In contrast, another variation tells of Orestes' death at the hand of the Taurean Artemis's high-priestess, who was in fact his sister Iphigenia, known also as the younger Hecate.[16] This account shows Artemis not as Apollo's cohort on Orestes' side but rather as his adversary. It also reveals her allegiance to the matriarchate, which colludes with Clytemnestra in revenge against Agamemnon. Graves describes such actions on the part of the goddess as

> one more incident in the feud between the house of Thyestes, assisted by Artemis, and the house of Atreus, assisted by Zeus. . . . It must be remembered that the Artemis who here measures her strength with Zeus is the earlier matriarchal Artemis, rather than Apollo's loving twin, the maiden huntress; the mythographers have done their best to obscure Apollo's active participation, on Zeus's side, in this divine quarrel.[17]

Here we get a glimpse into the occult relationship between Artemis and Apollo and see what lurks behind the veil of their patriarchal collusion. Theirs is an ambivalent relationship: partners on the one hand, adversaries on the other. And as in all deep relationships, real *coniunctio* derives less from the sameness of the two parties than from their differences. It is in their polarity, the tension of their opposition, that Artemis and Apollo can find their greatest creativity.

---

15 Ibid., vol. 2, p. 74.
16 Ibid., p. 78.
17 Ibid., p. 83.

They come to represent respectively the feminine and masculine principles. And as they confront one another, each is transformed, creating a third—the product of their union.

In this phase of the Cassandra woman's development, the imagery of father-daughter incest gives way to that of brother and sister. This may seem like going from the frying pan to the fire, but in fact it represents a progression.

As brother and sister, Artemis and Apollo are equal partners. She is a match for his power, ruthlessness and numinosity, whereas Cassandra had been overwhelmed by him. A dream of Sarah's illustrates the incestuous aspect of the relationship between the Artemis ego and the Apollo animus:

> I am in bed at night in the room I shared with my sister after I was eleven years old. Bugs in the thousands are coming through the window from the outside. I run in panic to my mother (who is in the room I had until I was eleven). But she doesn't care—she waves me off. Then I am lying in bed. I feel a strange force—a man, coming for me down the hall. I am terrified. I finally creep to the door and peer around it to see the horrible advancing shadow figure face to face. It is Tom [her brother]. Part of me is relieved, part is still terrified.

The context of this dream is puberty, the transition between latency and adolescence. The comradeship between Artemis and Apollo has heretofore been based on their sameness and a denial of their sexual differences. Now we see an emergence of the animus as other. The initial reaction of the ego is terror. Finally, in the dream, Sarah finds the courage to "peer" at the man, meaning both to look at and to be equal to him. She finds that he is none other than her brother, familiar but still terrifying.

This dream reflects a regressive, or at least conservative, tendency in which the woman would prefer to stay under the protective aegis of the mother-informed latency group. Likewise it reveals the dreamer's expectation that the mother, or the analyst as mother, will abandon her. It is very important at this point for the analyst to allow these rapprochements, listening to the analysand's fears and concerns but at the same time encouraging her to meet this otherness.

The feminine ego feels frightened and overwhelmed by the reemerging Apollonian animus. In the process of analysis, the Cassandra woman has experienced the trials of Demeter and Hecate, and her ego now has a firm footing in her own feminine identity. Nevertheless she is still in danger of becoming overidentified with, and consequently swept away by, the Apollonian animus.

Artemis herself was, on occasion, the victim of her brother, who was capable of taking selfish advantage of her sisterly devotion and betraying her naive trust in him. Did not Apollo, jealous of her affection for the beautiful hunter, Orion, trick Artemis into shooting him with her own bow and arrow?[18] This story hints at the underbelly of the relationship between the loving twins. Their state of merged identity gave Apollo the opportunity to manipulate Artemis. The goddess would have had to break their bond and take a stand against her brother, but she did not opt for such open conflict. Her typical modus operandi was to retreat to the protective precinct of her sacred grove and use her ultimate weapons only when cornered.

Sarah's dream indicates that retreat is no longer the answer. Interestingly, both she and Ellen had brothers with whom they had been, as with their fathers, collusively bonded. At this point for both of them, the relationship to the brother became focal and conflicted. They had unconsciously deferred to their brothers' opinions and wishes. Suddenly they found themselves infuriated and outraged by their brothers' attitudes, by the liberties taken and the lack of respect for their boundaries. It was very important for them now to claim their own reality, to say no to their brothers.

It may be time, in our modern age, for Artemis to risk letting slip her self-protective patriarchal persona and reach back into her identity as the primordial goddess, in order to stand over and against, as equal and opposite to Apollo. As Robert Graves suggests, what might be revealed is the aspect of Artemis that has never forgiven Apollo for his indignities against the feminine, and would have him remember his matriarchal roots.

This is the Artemis who would reduce Apollo to his pre-Hellenic, subordinate position as her high priest and consort. She would re-

---

18 Graves, *Greek Myths,* vol. 1, p. 152.

mind this sun-god of what he seems to have forgotten in his supremacy and his effort to avoid the devouring maw of matriarchal catabolism—that the sun must set at the end of the day.

Apollo will not willingly let go of his patriarchal supremacy. To the extent that he is still threatened by the goddess's power and afraid of her revenge, his best weapon is to keep his distance and continue to manipulate and use her for his own purposes.

Here we find a highly polarized situation. Artemis represents the archfeminine and Apollo the archmasculine. But there is also great potential for *coniunctio* since Apollo and Artemis are brother and sister—a tie that perhaps can bind and carry them through.

Artemis, the virgin huntress.
(Greek statue from Pompeii; Mansell Collection, London)

Themis as the Delphic oracle, seated on the tripod.
(Painted plate; Antikenabteilung, Berlin)

# 7

# Themis

*Leap for our Cities, and leap for our sea-borne ships, and leap
for our young citizens and for goodly Themis.*
                                    —The Hymn of the Kouretes.

In the patriarchal era, Artemis's and Apollo's defensive adaptation
was to deny their hostility and avoid conflict. They hid behind family
ties and retreated into their respective latency groups to protect and
consolidate their sexual identities.

But just as the adolescent emerges from the latency phase
interested in the other, so must Artemis and Apollo come out of their
narcissistic shells, admitting both their love and their hate for each
other and facing their incompleteness. She doesn't have a penis and
he doesn't have a womb. If they can mourn these facts and
acknowledge their envy, fear and desire, perhaps they can find what
they long for in each other. This requires both courage and
compromise. Retaining the shared attributes of their twinship—
adventurousness, integrity and the desire for truth—they must pro-
ceed in mutual vulnerability, trust and respect.

The love-hate relationship between Artemis and Apollo manifests
intrapsychically as intense conflict between ego and animus. The
woman may often be of two minds about an issue. The therapeutic
intention is to help her feel the split consciously by drawing up the
lines of battle as clearly as possible. One way this can be achieved is
through role-play and extensive dialogue concerning the different
points of view. Eventually the analysand will come to some middle
ground and experience the dynamic tension between polarity and
union.

In this phase a woman learns that there is great value in relating to
the other but also that she must not give herself over indiscriminately.
As she integrated the Artemis aspect into ego-consciousness, she
learned to say no on a very different basis from when she originally

131

rejected Apollo's advances. Now she is able to say it consciously. She knows her reasons and can do it with authority. The crucial next step is learning when to say yes.

Likewise, Apollo reemerges as animus in the psyche of the Cassandra woman, but on a new basis. He is no longer the ruling principle and center of the psyche. Early in the process, the ego disidentified from the patriarchal Apollonian animus and regressed to the maternal uroboric level. The animus, no longer fed by the psyche's libido, atrophied and regressed along with the ego. And just as ontogeny recapitulates phylogeny, the animus developed in the Cassandra woman along the same lines as Apollo's character changed historically: from the son-lover of the matriarchal goddess (Dionysus in the Hecate phase) through his heroic/Homeric form (Heracles in the Artemis phase) to the classical Apollo.

Now in this final phase Apollo can grow beyond the narcissistic misogynist who cursed Cassandra for rejecting him. The Apollonian animus has already experienced his own Dionysian shadow and has been mortified to some extent. Now he must learn to relate on equal footing to a strong feminine ego. He can no longer tyrannize her with blackmail and threats of abandonment. She has her own weapons, her own authority; she also knows how to make demands, be ruthless and wreak revenge. She is able to stand alone.

Furthermore, she is capable of creating a sacral space. This is a very important function, because now the ego can provide a container for the *coniunctio,* a holding environment for the psychic ebb and flow of union and separation.

The new Apollo must be able to tolerate rejection without lashing out in narcissistic rage. He too needs to be more receptive to the other, but he also needs to maintain his age-old ability to say no, in this case to feminine narcissism. Historically, this conservative function of classical Apollo is well known: he is propounder of the golden mean; teacher of "nothing in extreme, everything in moderation."

Apollo says no to the most atavistic and involutional aspects of the feminine. It is he who killed the Python, tamed the wild Muses, condemned Clytemnestra and banished the Furies. He decries the savagery and concretism of the matriarchy. He wants to put an end to the inexorable revenge cycle, asking for reflection on its horror and immorality. Apollo advocates forgiveness and transcendence and urges us to find the meaning of instinctual behavior rather than simply act it out. We can see his philosophy of purity and sublimity in the following excerpt from the Hymn to Apollo by the classical Hellenistic poet, Callimachus:

> Envy spoke secretly into the ear of Apollo,
> "I do not honor the singer who does not sing so great as is
>    the sea."
> Apollo kicked Envy with his foot and spoke thus:
> "The stream of the Assyrian river is great, but it bears
> In its waters much waste from the earth and much refuse.
> The bees do not carry to Deo just any water
> But what was pure and unsullied, a small, trickling stream
> From a sacred spring, its finest product."
> Hail, Lord. Ridicule and Envy away![1]

Here Apollo gives rise to an attack by Envy for distinguishing himself musically and also, perhaps, because of his holier-than-thou arrogance. But he defends himself quite well.

Envy constellates at this phase of the Cassandra woman's process in response to Apollo's reemergence in his classical form. As the ego begins to relate to and interact with the Apollonian animus, there may remain a shadow aspect which stubbornly refuses to be penetrated, preferring to remain in inflated identification with the Self. This is the power-mongering dominatrix, who wants only to control the male's phallic energy. She would rather destroy the patriarchal masculine than allow him to have any power of his own.

The Apollonian animus must pit himself against this evil aspect of the shadow lest it swallow up the entire psyche. This aspect of the feminine cannot be a part of *coniunctio,* for it resists compromise, sacrifice and an acceptance of limitation. Thus the envy that is felt in this phase is again oedipal, experienced by the disenfranchised third, the one who feels left out.

Insofar as the ego is still subject to infantile narcissism, this darkest aspect of the feminine can gain a foothold from which to work her

[1] Kerényi, *Apollo*, p. 26.

black magic. The animus may inform a woman of the kind of behavior he approves and disapproves, of what is appropriate or socially acceptable, but it is the ego that must do the work—make the choices, accept human limitations and suffer the consequences.

Sarah had a dream that illustrates both an ego ready to make the compromises necessary for *coniunctio* and also the narcissistic feminine shadow which resists it:

> I am in a sunny kitchen with a man and a woman who are my good friends. They are lovers and live together there. They are giving me a place to stay with them for awhile, and we talk about them helping me find a lover. I feel very good and protected. I go out in the backyard and find jewelry that has been dropped in the grass. It has been there a long time so that it's half in the ground and grass has grown up thickly around it. You can only find the pieces by feeling with your fingers. They are rings. One is my jade ring. I keep it. The others are Cassie's. One is a strange copy of my ring with a huge green crystal. I take the rings into the house where Cassie is sitting in a tub brim-full of water in a large room where the man and woman are also sitting. I drop the rings into the tub, telling Cassie that I found them. She picks them up, tells me she doesn't want them and throws them on the floor angrily, like a child having a tantrum. I pick them up and say patronizingly, "My, my! Aren't we in a snit!"

This dream of Sarah's recalls Ellen's dream of the kitchen in New York (page 123), but is a step further along. Here *coniunctio* has been consummated, the grandiose shadow has been mortified to some extent, and the couple is closer to ego-consciousness; that is, they are Sarah's good friends. They also have a parental quality. (It is not uncommon to see the constellation of good parents as an early *coniunctio* image).

This potential for union not only manifests intrapsychically, as an openness to the Apollonian animus, but can also be projected into life. It was at this time that Sarah expressed a desire for an ongoing relationship with a man and an interest in marriage and children.

The setting of the opening scene of the dream reflects the union of opposites in an abstract form: the kitchen representing the mother, the nourishing feminine container wherein transformation occurs, is permeated by the light of the sun, the solar consciousness of the spirit father.

It is within this precinct that Sarah finds the jewels, an image of the Self. A ring is a symbol of fidelity and commitment, of pledging troth. It holds the jade, which represents the hermaphroditic Self. In China, jade is known to possess a high degree of *yang,* the masculine principle. It is described as the solidified essence of pure mountain water, recalling the Hymn to Apollo. But jade has feminine *yin* qualities as well. Not only is it of the earth, but it is a very medial material, producing a rich, resonant, lingering tone when struck. Although very tough, jade is readily worked and can take a high polish. It was used in prehistoric times to manufacture weapons and utensils.[2] Thus it represents a practical aspect of the Self which can be utilized by the ego: artifice in its best sense.

In the dream, the jewels are still embedded in the earth; that is, they are still somewhat undifferentiated from the Great Mother. The dream ego has some work to do in order to mine them. First, she must feel with her fingers to extract them from the earth; in other words, she must use her embodied feeling function to know what is of value. Then she must deal with her infantile Cassie shadow who wants no part of the jewels.

Cassie is in the bathtub; therefore, psychologically, still in a narcissistic, preseparation state of merger with the feminine Self. She remains identified with the uroboric round, not yet able to relate to it symbolically as ring. Perhaps on some level she knows her ring is not as valuable as Sarah's, just as merger is a cheap imitation of *coniunctio.* Cassie's ring is crystal, a copy of the real thing, the precious stone. This reflects her use of magic rather than ego to get what she wants. Thus its color is the green of envy rather than of growth and fertility.

Of course, this is the same Cassie with whom Sarah had to "do things" in an earlier dream (page 119). Here, Cassie behaves (said Sarah) "like a bratty kid who wants to declare her dominance and

---

[2] *Funk & Wagnall's Standard Dictionary of Folklore, Mythology, and Legend,* p. 537.

show who is boss." This is the power drive that motivates the narcissistic shadow.

This dream makes it clear what Sarah needs to do with Cassie. Her healthy ego already has access to the Apollonian animus. Now, with a firm but caring parental attitude, she must face her own narcissistic shadow which continues to sabotage her and keeps her from claiming what is of great value.

The reward for taming the narcissistic shadow, working through oedipal envy and accepting the need to compromise, is the further disidentification of ego from Self and the differentiation of personal and transpersonal shadow. The ego does not lose a mother, it gains a partner: an animus which enables her to apprehend symbolic reality and lends propriety, decorum, formality and aesthetic sensibility. Here the animus behaves like what Freud called the superego.

The new animus also functions to orient the ego to the outside world. This is Apollo, god of the *polis,* the law, founder of ordinances which give society its form. It was to Apollo that Plato gave the responsibility of deciding all religious and moral questions in his ideal republic.

Even archfeminist Christa Wolf recognizes Apollo's value and that we cannot simply go back to nature, back to matriarchal times: "'Know thyself,' the maxim of the Delphic oracle, . . . is one of Apollo's slogans; it could not have occurred to any goddess in the undifferentiated age."[3] After all, why should we disavow ourselves of four thousand years of development? Granted the feminine has suffered greatly during the patriarchal age, but the answer is not to regress only to begin another cycle of revenge. We must instead attempt to distill out the best of the patriarchy.

Walter Otto describes the value of Apollonian consciousness in the following passage, which concerns one of the most important attributes of the god, namely distance:

On the surface this word expresses only something negative, but its implication is something most positive—the attitude of cognition. Apollo objects to extreme proximity, the self-consciousness of things, the blurred gaze, and equally the spiritual exchange, the mystical inebriation and its ecstatic dream. He wants not soul (in the

---

[3] Wolf, *Cassandra,* p. 294.

Dionysiac sense) but spirit. In Apollo we encounter the spirit of observable knowledge which stands in antithesis to existence and to the world with unequalled freedom—the genuine Greek spirit which was destined to produce not merely so many arts but ultimately even science.[4]

As Apollo reconstellates within the analytic container, there is a change in the role of the analyst, especially in the way her own animus operates. In the Hecate phase when the analyst was working out of her Dionysian animus, therapeutic intervention involved mainly mirroring and confrontation of the analysand's behavior in concrete, descriptive terms. Now the interpretations are more symbolic, analytical. Here Apollo reveals himself in his best classical form, seeking rational understanding, clarity, objectivity, perspective. To the extent that the analysand's ego is still identified with the dark side of the feminine, she may resist such interpretations.

Ellen's dream describes this resistance:

I am asleep in a room with pine paneling—either at camp or a youth hostel. I am awakened by a doctor in a white coat who wants to give me an injection. I think, "He shouldn't be here." I try to run away but another man grabs me from behind, around my throat.

Here we see the dream ego still identified with Artemis's wild nature, resisting penetration by the animus—in this case, Apollo as god of medicine. This dream came at the end of a month-long summer hiatus and revealed a negative transference reaction to resuming therapy. The second man represents the heroic animus, already firmly entrenched in her psyche. This is the same figure who restrained the dogs in her earlier dream (page 121). Here he grips Ellen around the throat—as Heracles did Cerberus in the myth—holding her down so that the doctor/analyst/Apollonian animus can treat her.

No doubt Ellen experienced all of this as a gang rape by the masculine elements in her psyche, but there is an implication, in her association to the pine paneling as "coffinlike," that something vital will die if she is unable to give up her feminine narcissism.

---

[4] Walter Otto, *The Homeric Gods,* p. 78.

The following dream of Jane's shows what the Cassandra woman stands to gain by acknowledging her narcissistic shadow and working through oedipal issues.

I volunteer my services as a teacher at a school, while they go through a transition. I am assigned to a class of preschool children (4 to 5 year olds). I look forward to it. . . . Later there is an open house on campus to show the changes that have been made. I wander through the grounds. There are gorgeous trees and flowers. I'm walking on the beautifully manicured green lawn. I come to a stone wall. The lawn extends on from the top of the wall, like a plateau. A man standing on the lawn above helps me up the wall to his level. I recognize him—he is the guest of honor. . . . On the way home, I am invited to join a group of seven other people, one of whom is this man. And I will be the eighth. It will be some kind of psychological experiment. I am interested.

The setting of this dream is a school, a place dedicated to education, the furthering of knowledge and cognition. Like Sarah, Jane must work with the oedipal child. This is the age when children have their first life experiences outside the home. Although Jane did not attend kindergarten at the school referred to in the dream, she did spend her happiest and most successful adolescent years there. This association, plus her positive attitude, bodes well for her accomplishing the task assigned by her psyche.

In the dream this work leads to a transformation on the campus. First there is a flourishing of the natural environment, suggesting that the psychological changes are pleasing not only to the god of logos but also to Mother Earth, who is not behaving here like a narcissistic matriarch atavistically resisting any input from the spirit god. For the grounds in the dream are highly cultivated, the lawns and gardens finely manicured, indicating a union of heaven and earth.

The changes also include the reappearance of the Apollonian animus. This man, the guest of honor, reminded Jane of two teachers she had in school: one had taught her art/art history in high school; the other was a college biology professor who particularly impressed her with his interest in the limbic system, which connects psyche and soma. Both teachers had been fair-haired, attractive young men with the qualities of clarity, objectivity and aesthetic sensibility. Thus the dream figure represents an animus informed by Apollo, god of art and science, for whom the dreamer holds the proper attitude of honor and respect rather than fearful resistance.

This new Apollonian animus, like the two teachers, extends himself in a helpful, related manner, with no strings attached; that is, he no longer demands mirroring and obeisance. Now he is an esteemed colleague.

The man helps Jane overcome the obstacle of the stone wall and reach a higher level. A stone wall is used to bound private property; it is also a colloquial expression for an obstruction. Thus, psychologically, it represents the clear-cut ego boundaries so important for the Cassandra woman to erect in the Artemis phase. But these rigid boundaries can become the armor for the narcissistic aspect and thus an obstruction to further development. The wall's three-footedness suggests the oedipal nature of the obstruction. The transformed Apollonian animus helps the ego to sublimate the regressive oedipal longings and rise above the concretistic, defensive, earthbound quality of the Artemis phase, while still remaining grounded.

This is a very important step for the Cassandra woman, whose very nature demands that at times she have the capacity to transcend her own ego limits. If she can appreciate the Apollonian animus, what was once for her a stone wall can transform into another three-foot object—the tripod, upon which the Pythia sat to receive her divine inspiration. Here we have a beautiful illustration of how the third element in the oedipal triangle can become the *tertium non datur,* the third not logically given, the product of the *coniunctio.* Even the design of the tripod bespeaks union:

> It was formed of a serpent of bronze, coiled spirally upwards in the form of a cone, and terminating in three heads. As the cone or pyramid was a symbol of the sun's rays, this typified the union of the worship of Apollo, the Sun-god, with that of the Serpent, the Python, or earth deity.[5]

At the beginning of her process, the Cassandra woman had no ego vessel with which to receive Apollo. In the course of analysis, she has developed a womb which can hold, which no longer wanders.

---

[5] Howie, *Encircled Serpent,* p. 143.

She has undergone transformation and is ready to receive the animus. Now that she has a strong vessel, she can assume her role as Pythia and be a medium for his inspiration.

Her ego is the medium. The Apollonian animus carries the message, the Logos Spermaticos, the fertilizing spirit which comes to her through the ether. Her medial instrument, that body/mind/emotional complex we call the feminine ego, picks up and vibrates with the message. She smells it, feels it, senses it, holding these kinesthetic impressions, gestating them until a gestalt forms.

In the past, she would have become hysterical. In fear and anxiety, she would have blurted out her unmetabolized impressions, meeting with disbelief on all sides. Now she can hold the contents until they are fully cooked. Then the animus can help her to understand cognitively and symbolically what she sees and feels. Finally the animus helps her to articulate what needs to be communicated, to discriminate where and when to do so and even to express herself in a refined aesthetic form, like the Delphic priest who interpreted the Pythia's utterances and translated them into poetry. Thus the Cassandra woman delivers her oracle. She can now believe in her perceptions and be believed by others.

The following illustrates the evolution of the Cassandra woman from medium to mediatrix. After several years of individual analysis, Sarah became a member of my ongoing therapy group. At first, the psychic split between Apollonian animus and Cassandra shadow was markedly present. When she was securely identified with her Apollonian animus/ego, she was in control and on top of things. She talked about herself objectively and offered insightful, albeit somewhat superficial and unrelated, interpretations to the other members.

But every now and then, when some dark perception came up about herself or another, she would be overwhelmed by the morbid complex. At these times she was like another person, no longer strong and self-assured. She would look terrified, horror-struck, crying or speaking incomprehensibly and impressionistically. This only induced confusion and frustration, even sadistic attack, in the rest of the group. Then Sarah would retreat, speechless and paralyzed.

As she learned to contain and process her medial perceptions, Sarah became one of the group's most esteemed members, valued and respected—though somewhat feared—for her penetrating insights and judgments. She had a real gift for seeing what was going on beneath the surface in herself and others, as well as the dynamics of the group as a whole. She displayed a high degree of collective consciousness.

But what is the archetypal dominant underlying this phase of ego development? The illustration opposite the opening of this chapter shows Aegeus, father of Theseus, consulting the oracle. The Pythia is seated on the tripod, holding a laurel sprig in her right hand and a vessel of holy water in her left. This represents the union of masculine and feminine and the need for both Apollo and the mother goddess to cooperate in the practice of divination. Here, the Pythia is Themis herself, "second from her mother [Gaia] .../ to be seated on this sybil's chair."[6] Classical scholar Jane Harrison describes Themis as the spirit of the oracle. "Gods might come and go, Gaia and Phoibe and Phoibos, but Themis who . . . is below and above all gods abides there seated."

As in Jane's dream (page 138), once the animus helps the ego up to a higher level, we have left the realm of Artemis and entered that of Themis, ultimate patroness of the Cassandra woman and a symbol, par excellence, of both virginity and *coniunctio*. As the daughter of Gaia and Uranus, Themis is the product of the union between heaven and earth, but she is also a triple goddess and titaness of the planet Jupiter in her own right.[7] Aeschylus, who envisaged her as the oracular power of Earth, considered her to be identical with her mother: "Themis, and Gaia, one in nature, many-named."[8]

Themis did not avoid the company of men. Not only was she the natural mother of Evander, by Hermes, and surrogate mother for the infant Apollo, feeding him on nectar and ambrosia, but Themis was also a partner.[9] She shared the titanship of Jupiter with Eurymedon,

---

[6] Aeschylus, *The Orestes Plays*, p. 159.

[7] Graves, *Greek Myths*, vol. 1, pp. 27, 324.

[8] Harrison, *Themis*, p. 480.

[9] Graves, *Greek Myths*, vol. 1, p. 76; vol. 2, p. 137.

and later became the second wife of Zeus. "She who was of earth, she who was Earth herself, leaves her home and goes the way of all things divine, up to Olympos. . . . an alien kingdom," where she is seated beside Zeus, wife and advisor.[10] Together they bore the Seasons and planned the Trojan War, possibly to decrease the surplus population.[11]

But Themis was more than the help-meet of Zeus. Even on Olympus she had power of her own. She bore the important function of calling the gods and demigods to council.[12] Likewise, it was her job to convene and dissolve the agora (assembly of citizens) and to preside over sacramental feasts.[13] Thus, psychologically, Themis represents the capacity of the feminine ego to gather up and hold the contents and forces of the collective unconscious until their meaning can be understood and integrated. This Themis function enables the Cassandra woman to fulfill the ultimate mandate of her psyche—to be mediatrix instead of medium for the collective, and interpreter of the Zeitgeist.

Jane's dream describes the ego's task and shows how the animus can help; it also reveals the potential result of this joint work by ego and animus, namely the unknown, unexpected product of the union of opposites—the group of eight, a doubling of the quaternity. If four symbolizes the wholeness of the Self, then this eightfold quality expands on its collective nature. *Coniunctio* becomes community. Individuation is no longer the end-point and supreme goal of psychic growth. The concept of superego takes on transpersonal dimensions.

Jane's association to the "psychological experiment" in the dream was a scene from Jean Auel's novel, *The Clan of the Cave Bear.* In a drug-induced trance, the magicians of a Cro-Magnon clan partake in a ritual in which they pass around the skull and eat the brain of a hunter killed by the clan's totem, the cave bear. The following passage describes their communal experience through the eyes of Ayla, a Neanderthal woman adopted by the Clan:

---

10 Harrison, *Themis,* p. 519.
11 Graves, *Greek Myths,* vol. 2, p. 269.
12 Harrison, *Themis,* p. 482.
13 Ibid., p. 482.

She sensed emotions alien to her, emotions not her own. Strongest was love, but mixed in was deep anger and great fear, and then a hint of curiosity. With a shock, she realized Mog-ur [the chief magician] was inside her head. In her mind, she felt his thoughts, with her emotions, his feelings. There was a distinctly physical quality to it, a sense of crowding without its unpleasantness, more like a touching that was closer than physical touching.

The mind-altering roots . . . accentuated a natural tendency of the Clan. Instinct had evolved, in Clan people, into memory. But memory, taken far enough back, became identical, became racial memory. The racial memories of the Clan were the same; and with perceptions sensitized, they could share their identical memories. . . .

She knew the profound sense of reverence with which the magicians had indulged in the cannibalistic act that had so revolted her. She hadn't realized, she had no way of knowing, that it was a communion. The reason for the Gathering of the clans was to bind them together, to make them Clan. . . . All Clan people shared a common heritage, and remembered it, and any ritual performed at any one Gathering had the same significance for all. The magicians believed they were making a beneficial contribution to the Clan. They were absorbing the courage of the young man who was journeying with the Spirit of Ursus.[14]

In a trance state, Ayla traces the racial memory not only back in time but also into the future where she sees the two lines of prehistoric man, Cro-Magnon and Neanderthal, merge to become homo sapiens. This story is Auel's fantasy, or I should say memory, of prehistoric existence. What she describes is exceedingly primitive, nonetheless it can provide a symbolic model for what we, with our drive toward individuation and exogamy, need to reclaim.

While communal experience might appear to be a step backward to a primitive level of functioning, it actually represents, in the manner of alpha and omega, an evolutionary step forward for those who stand at the brink of the Aquarian Age. A sense of community is imperative lest we destroy Mother Earth.

---

[14] *The Clan of the Cave Bear,* pp. 424-427.

It may seem that we have wandered far afield from Themis, but actually this kind of collective consciousness lies well within her realm. In 1927, Jane Harrison wrote:

> Themis was . . . at first of the tribe, and then she was all powerful. Later when the tribal system, through wars and incursions and migrations, broke up, its place was taken less dominantly, more effectively, by the *polis*. The *polis* set itself to modify and inform all those primitive impulses and instincts that are resumed in Earth-worship. It also set itself, if unconsciously, as a counterbalance to the dominance of ties of near kinship. . . .
>
> Themis convenes the assembly. . . . she is the very spirit of the assembly incarnate. Themis and the actual concrete agora are barely distinguishable. . . .
>
> Here the social fact is trembling on the very verge of godhead. She is the force that brings and binds men together, she is "herd instinct," the collective conscience, the social sanction. She is *fas*, the social imperative. This social imperative is among a primitive group diffuse, vague, inchoate, yet absolutely binding. Later it crystallizes into fixed conventions, regular tribal customs; finally in the *polis* it takes shape as Law and Justice. Themis was before the particular shapes of gods; she is not religion, but she is the stuff of which religion is made. It is the emphasis and representation of herd instinct, of the collective conscience, that constitutes religion. . . .
>
> Religion sums up and embodies what we feel together, what we care for together, what we imagine together. . . .
>
> It is when religion ceases to be a matter of feeling together, when it becomes individualized and intellectualized, that clouds gather on the horizon.[15]

In part one, we learned that Cassandra's plight had its roots in the collective conflict of her times, dramatized by Aeschylus in *The Eumenides* as the battle of the sexes. In the play Athena, who gave allegiance to the new patriarchal order, resolved the struggle between matriarchal and patriarchal law. Now, two thousand years later, we can see that Aeschylus' *dea ex machina* was only an interim solution. The Furies were not permanently appeased by Athena's unkept promise of respect. The battle has continued throughout the last

---

[15] *Themis*, pp. 484-487.

aion—occasionally as open conflict, sometimes as guerilla warfare, more often as underground activity.

Now we need a more balanced resolution. For the modern Cassandra woman, in whom the battle of the sexes still rages, a reconciling image can be found in Themis, the quintessential product of *coniunctio*. Themis "begins on earth and ends in heaven."[16] But never in her evolution, even as she survived in the patriarchy, did she lose her original identity as the embodiment of both mantic wisdom and collective justice.

Themis has lived under matriarchal *and* patriarchal law. She represents the best aspects of both. She is offended when human action violates law. But she is also offended when statutory law is not grounded in consensus or is not in harmony with the natural order of the universe. Themis reflects the fairness and objectivity of masculine law without its overly-abstract purity of law for law's sake—which in our own legal system, for example, allows the guilty to get off on a technicality or the innocent to rot in prison if they are too poor or ignorant to fight for their rights. This goddess stands for the spirit rather than the letter of the law.

Likewise, Themis embodies the discriminating—even searing— judgment of feminine law, which is practical and related, *ad hominem*. This is extraverted feeling in its best sense, without the concretistic reactivity of matriarchal revenge. She has a true eye which sees both near and far, and she can turn her vision deeply inward or out into the cosmos.

---

[16] Ibid., p. 483.

The Themis of Rhamnus.
(National Museum, Athens)

# Seeing is Believing

Man or woman, we are all medial to some degree. Mediality is a messy, often painful affair. What we make of it depends upon many factors.

We have seen that although the medial woman is driven to express the shadow aspects of her culture, she remains personally responsible for the consequences of her own psyche.

On the other hand, just as a dream belongs to the collective, so does medial knowledge. We no longer have institutions to honor and utilize mediality, as did the ancients. Therefore we must, as individuals, be open to the collective value of the messages that come through ourselves and others.

The stakes are a lot higher today than in Cassandra's time. On the negative side, we can destroy everything with the push of a button. Thus, actions taken in one small corner can have global repercussions. But on the positive side, the message of hope whispered by a single voice can be transmitted to all.

Honoring the medial is tantamount psychologically to consulting an oracle. Jane Harrison writes that this involves "a veritable, almost physical, *rite de passage*. . . . The suppliant must pass out of the actual, sensible, 'objective' world, into that other world of dream, of ecstasy, of trance."[1] Thus the medial experience is an initiation process, entailing a death and rebirth, during which we pass into the region of taboo and then return to re-member what we saw. What is required is an attitude of receptivity to the unconscious, to irrational otherness. Such an attitude is practically inaccessible to the ego identified with patriarchal values.

Several years ago, while traveling in Europe, I noticed a man in the lobby of my hotel reading Christa Wolf's *Cassandra*. In the course of a conversation with him, I asked what he thought Cassandra's problem was. He surprised me with his answer that the people were too blind and narrow-minded to believe her. I thought to

---

[1] Harrison, *Themis,* p. 512.

myself, "How simplistic. Doesn't he understand that the onus was on her?"

At the time I was deeply involved in the process of dissecting and analyzing Cassandra's psyche, with an eye to how the modern Cassandra woman can personally integrate her medial aspect. How ironic that I played the disbelieving chorus to this man's Cassandra.

Now I see the truth in what this stranger had to say. A Cassandra woman may be able to ground her hysterical shadow and integrate her medial aspect into ego-consciousness, coming to firmly believe what she sees and knows. She may reach the level of development where she has internalized the positive Apollonian animus and can express her insight in a clear, objective way.

Nonetheless, she may still not be believed. Because of their source in the collective shadow, her prophecies are seditious; they threaten the conservative order. Thus she speaks treason. Until the intrinsic value of mediality can be accepted, we shall continue to attack her for bearing bad tidings.

We must be aware, however, that in many cases she bears true witness and neither she, nor we, can any longer afford to disbelieve. The Cassandra woman who has escaped the curse of the patriarchal Apollo speaks for a new age.

Themis corresponds to Tarot Trump VIII, Adjustment, representing Libra, also called Justesse—"assessing the virtue of every act and demanding exact and precise satisfaction."—from The Master Therion (Alistair Crowley), *The Book of Thoth* (New York: Samuel Weiser, 1974).

unfortunate choice
to illustrate the point undermines
her ideas.

# Glossary of Jungian Terms

**Anima** (Latin, "soul"). The unconscious, feminine side of a man's personality. She is personified in dreams by images of females ranging from child to seductress to spiritual guide. A man's anima development is reflected in how he relates to women.

**Animus** (Latin, "spirit"). The unconscious, masculine side of a woman's personality. A negative animus can cause a women to be rigid, opinionated and argumentative. The animus is personified in women's dreams by images ranging from muscle-men to poets to spiritual leaders. A woman's animus development is reflected in how she relates to men.

**Archetypes.** Irrepresentable in themselves, archetypes appear in consciousness as **archetypal images** and ideas. These are universal patterns or motifs present in the collective unconscious, the basic content of religion, mythology, legends and art.

**Association.** Spontaneous flow of interconnected thoughts and images around a specific idea.

**Complex.** An emotionally charged group of ideas or images. At the core of a complex is an archetype or archetypal image.

**Constellate.** Whenever there is a strong emotional reaction to a person or a situation, a complex has been constellated (activated).

**Coniunctio.** A term from alchemy, referring to the coming together of opposites. It corresponds to a condition of psychological wholeness, a state in which ego-consciousness and the unconscious work together in harmony.

**Ego.** The central complex of consciousness. A strong ego can relate objectively to activated contents of the unconscious (i.e., other complexes) rather than identifying with them.

**Feeling.** One of the four psychic functions in Jung's model of personality types. It is a *rational* function which evaluates the worth of relationships and situations. The feeling function is different from emotion, which results from the activation of a complex.

**Identification.** See below, **participation mystique.**

150

**Individuation.** The conscious realization of one's unique psychological reality, including both strengths and limitations. It leads to the experience of the **Self** as the regulating center of the psyche.

**Inflation.** A state in which one has an unrealistically high or low (negative inflation) sense of self-worth.

**Intuition.** One of the four psychic functions. In Jung's model of personality types, it is an *irrational* function which picks up, via the unconscious, future potentialities inherent in the present.

**Participation mystique.** A primitive, unconscious connection in which one cannot clearly distinguish oneself from the other (people or things). This is what lies behind the phenomenon of **projection.**

**Persona** (Latin, "actor's mask"). One's social role, derived from the expectations of society and early training. A persona is useful both in facilitating contact with others and as a protective covering.

**Projection.** A natural process whereby an unconscious quality or characteristic of one's own is perceived and reacted to in an outer object or person.

**Self.** The archetype of wholeness and the regulating center of the psyche. It is experienced as a numinous transpersonal power which transcends the ego (e.g., God).

**Sensation.** The second *irrational* function in Jung's model. It perceives immediate, physical reality.

**Shadow.** A mainly unconscious part of the personality, characterized by traits and attitudes, both negative and positive, which the conscious ego tends to reject or ignore. It is personified in dreams by persons of the same sex as the dreamer.

**Symbol.** The best possible expression for something essentially unknown. Symbolic thinking is wholistic, right-brain oriented; it is complementary to logical, linear, left-brain thinking.

**Tertium non datur.** The reconciling third that emerges from the unconscious (in the form of a symbol or a new attitude) after the tension between conflicting opposites has been held.

**Transference-countertransference.** Similar to projection, used to describe the unconscious, emotional bonds that arise in a therapeutic relationship.

# Selected Bibliography

Aeschylus. *The Agamemnon.* Trans. Gilbert Murray. London: George Allen & Unwin, 1920.

_____. *The Eumenides.* Trans. Gilbert Murray. London: George Allen & Unwin, 1925.

_____. *The Orestes Plays.* Trans. Paul Roche. New York: New American Library, 1962.

Auel, Jean. *The Clan of the Cave Bear.* New York: Bantam Books, 1980.

Berlioz, Hector. *Les Troyens.* Libretto of opera after Virgil. 1858.

Bird, Virginia. *Artemis Alive.* Unpublished Thesis, C.G. Jung Institute of New York, 1981.

Dale-Green, Patricia. *The Archetypal Cat.* Originally published as *Cult of the Cat.* Boston: Houghton Mifflin, 1963; reprint ed., Dallas: Spring Publications, n.d.

*Diagnostic and Statistical Manual of Mental Disorders* (DSM II). Washington: American Psychiatric Association, 1968.

Dodds, E. R. *The Greeks and the Irrational.* Berkeley: University of California Press, 1956.

Ehrenwald, Jan. *The E.S.P. Experience: A Psychiatric Validation.* New York: Basic Books, 1978.

Euripedes. *Trojan Women.* Trans. Gilbert Murray. London: George Allen & Unwin, 1906.

Farnell, Lewis R. *The Cults of the Greek States,* vol. 4. Oxford: Clarendon Press, 1907.

Fenichel, Otto. *The Psychoanalytic Theory of Neurosis.* New York: Norton & Co., 1945.

Flacelière, Robert. *Greek Oracles.* London: Elek Books, 1965.

Fontenrose, Joseph. *The Delphic Oracle.* Berkeley: University of California Press, 1978.

_____. *Python: A Study of Delphic Myth and Its Origin.* Berkeley, University of California Press, 1959.

Frey-Rohn, Liliane. *From Freud to Jung.* New York: G.P. Putnam's Sons, for the C. G. Jung Foundation for Analytical Psychology, 1974.

*Funk & Wagnalls Standard Dictionary of Folklore, Mythology, and Legend.* San Francisco: Harper & Row, 1972.

Gordon, Rosemary. "The Concept of Projective Identification." *Journal of Analytical Psychology,* vol. 10, no. 2 (July 1965), pp. 127-149.

152

Graves, Robert. *The Greek Myths,* vols. 1 and 2. Middlesex, England: Penguin Books, 1955, revised ed., 1960.

Hamilton, Edith. *Mythology.* New York: New American Library, 1940.

Harding, M. Esther. *Woman's Mysteries.* New York: G. P. Putnam's Sons, for the C.G. Jung Foundation for Analytical Psychology, 1971.

Harrison, Jane. *Themis: A Study of the Social Origins of Greek Religion.* Cambridge: University Press, 1927.

Hillman, James. *The Myth of Analysis.* New York: Harper Colophon Books, 1978.

Homer. *The Iliad.* Trans. W. H. D. Rouse. New York: New American Library, 1938.

Howie, M. Oldfield. *The Cat in the Mysteries of Religion and Magic.* New York: Castle Books, 1956.

_____. *The Encircled Serpent.* London: Ryder & Co., 1926.

Jung, C.G. *The Collected Works* (Bollingen Series XX). 20 vols. Trans. R.F.C. Hull. Ed. H. Read, M. Fordham, G. Adler, Wm. McGuire. Princeton: Princeton University Press, 1973.

Jung, C.G. and Kerényi, K. *Essays on a Science of Mythology.* Princeton: Princeton University Press, 1949.

Kerényi, K. *Apollo.* Dallas: Spring Publications, 1983.

_____. *Dionysus.* Princeton: Princeton University Press, 1976.

Kernberg, Otto. "Psychoanalytic Psychotherapy with Borderline and Narcissistic Patients." Lecture, Cape Cod Institute, Albert Einstein College of Medicine, Dept. of Psychiatry, Aug. 23-27, 1982.

Klein, Melanie. *Envy and Gratitude.* (1963). New York: Dell Publishing Co., 1977.

Lagerkvist, Pär. *The Sybil.* New York: Vintage Books, 1958.

*Larousse Encyclopedia of Mythology.* London: Hamlyn Publishing, 1968.

May, Rollo. *The Courage to Create.* Toronto: Bantam Books, 1976.

Micklem, Neil. "On Hysteria: The Mythical Syndrome." *Spring 1974.*

Neumann, Erich. *The Great Mother: An Analysis of the Archetype* (Bollingen Series XLVII). Trans. Ralph Manheim. Princeton: Princeton University Press, 1963.

_____. *The Origins and History of Consciousness* (Bollingen Series XLII). Trans. R.F.C. Hull. Princeton: Princeton University Press, 1954.

Otto, Walter F. *The Homeric Gods.* Boston: Beacon Press, 1954.

Perera, Sylvia Brinton. *Descent to the Goddess: A Way of Initiation for Women.* Toronto: Inner City Books, 1981.

Pollard, John. *Seers, Shrines, and Sirens.* London: George Allen & Unwin, 1965.

Quenk, Alex. "Hysteria: A Dynamic and Clinical Entity." Proceedings of the Inter-Regional Society of Jungian Analysts, Fall 1978.

Rohde, Edward. *Psyche.* London: Harcourt Brace & Co., 1925.

Segal, Hannah. *Introduction to the Work of Melanie Klein.* 2nd ed. New York: Basic Books, 1980.

Shapiro, David. *Neurotic Styles.* New York: Basic Books, 1965.

Spignesi, Angelyn."Toward a Psychological Understanding of the Witch." Published in Italian: "Verso una Comprensione Psicologica della Strega." *Giornale Storica di Psicologica Dinamica,* vol. 7 (1983).

Starhawk. *The Spiral Dance: A Rebirth of the Ancient Religion of the Great Goddess.* New York: Harper & Row, 1979.

Veith, Ilza. *Hysteria: The History of a Disease.* Chicago: University of Chicago Press, 1965.

Vernant, Jean-Pierre. *Myth and Thought among the Greeks.* London: Routledge & Kegan Paul, 1983.

Wasson, R. Gordon; Ruck, Carl A. P.; Hofmann, Albert. *The Road to Eleusis.* New York: Harcourt Brace Jovanovich, 1978.

Whitmont, Edward C. *Return of the Goddess.* London: Routledge & Kegan Paul, 1983.

Williams, Mary. "A Study of Hysteria in Women." *Journal of Analytical Psychology,* vol. 2 (1956).

Wolf, Christa. *Cassandra: A Novel and Four Essays.* New York: Farrar, Straus & Giroux, 1984.

Wolff, Toni. "Structural Forms of the Feminine Psyche." Monograph privately printed for the Students' Association, C. G. Jung Institute of Zurich, 1956.

Woodman, Marion. *The Pregnant Virgin: A Process of Psychological Transformation.* Toronto: Inner City Books, 1985.

# Index